LUCINDA GUY

CROCHET DESIGNS

FOR GIRLS AND BOYS

LUCINDA GUY
CROCHET DESIGNS
FOR GIRLS AND BOYS

Illustrations by François Hall

ROWAN

A Rowan publication

First published in 2008 by
Rowan Yarns
Green Lane Mill
Holmfirth
West Yorkshire
England
HD9 2DX

Designs by Lucinda Guy
Photography, illustrations and layout by François Hall
Editor Sally Harding
Technical consultant/pattern writer Penny Hill
Pattern checker Tricia Mckenzie

British Library Cataloguing in Publication Data
A catalogue record for this book is available from the
British Library.

ISBN 978-1-906007-35-5

Printed in China

CONTENTS

INTRODUCTION

The projects in this book are designed to inspire you to make wonderful and original things in very simple crochet for small kids to wear, use and play with.

All the projects are suitable for both the beginner and more experienced crocheter alike, because only simple double or treble crochet or easy-to-learn fancier stitches are used. Whilst some of the garments can be made really quickly — such as the Summer Cap, Winter Warmers and the Posy Headscarf — other projects, although essentially simple to crochet, will take a little longer and need just that extra bit of patience to assemble, such as the Bon-Bon Blanket or the Ariadne Doll.

If you are concerned that even these projects are not simple enough, remember that you can simplify them yourself. For example, you do not have to make the motifs for the garments — Milo for the Milo Owl Jumper, Marcel the Snail for the striped top, Bessie Bird for the coat or the posies for the Posy Pinafore. You could also omit any stripes or embroidery and just make a plain garment. Obviously, I think that this would be a shame as these are the elements that bring the garments alive and make them stand apart from the ordinary. However, these details are not there to put you off!

So simplify if you must and change the colours to suit you, but above all, do be inspired and try some crochet!

SPRING

Soft, sweet and gentle for spring, all these easily made designs are crocheted in a classic pure wool 4-ply that is machine washable.

Posy Pinafore (page 10)

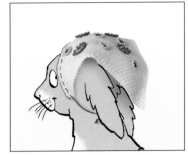

Posy Headscarf (page 16)

Marcel the Snail Top (page 20)

Little Stripy Bag (page 24)

Bon-Bon blanket (page 26)

SUMMER

Light, airy and ideal for summer dressing, these simple projects are made in fine 4-ply cotton that is also machine washable. Perfect!

Sweet Cicely Skirt (page 30)

Sweet Cicely Top (page 34)

Summer Cap (page 38)

Wilbur Whale (page 42)

Best Beach Bag (page 48)

AUTUMN

Pure wools in 4-ply or DK are used for these easy and wonderful designs. Machine washable, they are not only stylish but also practical.

Dolores Dress (page 52)

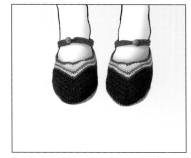

Dolores Slippers (page 58)

Ariadne Doll (page 62)

Annie Overblouse (page 68)

Cosy Connie Jumper (page 72)

WINTER

Cosy, warm pure DK wool is used to make these comforting winter woollies. Easy to make, easy to use and wear, easily machine washable.

Bessie Bird Coat (page 76)

Milo Owl Jumper (page 86)

Winter Warmers (page 92)

Henri Elephant (page 96)

Zigzag Throw (page 104)

POSY PINAFORE

Sweet and lovely, this little pinafore
is a must-have for spring. Keep it
plain and simple with just a belt and
buckle or decorate the pockets with
little flowers and pearly buttons.
Then wear it with the headscarf on
page 17 and the bag on page 25.

page 17 and the bag on page 25.

BEFORE YOU BEGIN

SIZES AND MEASUREMENTS

To fit ages (in years)	2–3	3–4	4–5
To fit chest	56cm	61cm	66cm
	22in	24in	26in
Finished measurements			
Around chest	68cm	74cm	79cm
	26¾in	29in	31in
Length to shoulder	50cm	56cm	64cm
	19¾in	22in	25¼in

YARN

Rowan *4-Ply Soft* (50g/1¾ oz balls) as follows:

A	pink (Fairy 395)	3 balls	4 balls	4 balls
B	red (Honk 374)	2 balls	2 balls	2 balls
C	sage green (Leafy 367)	1 ball	1 ball	1 ball
D	pale blue (Whisper 370)	1 ball	1 ball	1 ball

HOOK

2.50mm (US size C-2) crochet hook

EXTRAS

2 mother-of-pearl buttons 2cm/¾in in diameter,
to fasten straps on pinafore
6 small buttons for flower centres (optional)
1 buckle

TENSION

25 sts and 26 rows to 10cm/4in measured over dc
using 2.50mm (US size C-2) crochet hook *or size
necessary to obtain correct tension*.

ABBREVIATIONS

dc2tog = [insert hook in next st, yrh and draw
a loop through] twice, yrh and draw through all
3 loops on hook — *one st decreased*.
See also page 110.

See also page 110.

PINAFORE

FRONT

Using 2.50mm (US size C-2) hook and B, make
109 (121: 133) ch.
Fasten off.
Change to A on next row as follows:
Foundation row (RS) Join A with a ss to first ch,
1 ch (does NOT count as a st), 1 dc in same
place as ss, 1 dc in each of rem ch, turn. *109
(121: 133) dc.*
Row 1 (patt row) 1 ch (does NOT count as a
st), 1 dc in each dc to end, turn.
(Last row forms simple dc patt when repeated.)
Cont in dc throughout, work 2 rows more.
Next row (dec row) (RS) 1 ch, 1 dc in each of
first 6 dc, work dc2tog over next 2 dc, 1 dc in
each dc to last 8 dc, work dc2tog over next 2 dc,
1 dc in each of last 6 dc, turn.
Work straight for 3 rows, ending with a WS row.
Rep last 4 rows 13 (15:17) times more and then
the dec row again. *79 (87: 95) dc.*
Work straight until Front measures 25 (30:
35)cm/9¾ (11¾: 13¾) in from beg, ending with a
RS row.
Next row (WS) 1 ch, 1 dc in each of first 2 dc,
[1 dc in each of next 6 dc, work dc2tog over next
2 dc] 9 (10: 11) times, work dc2tog over next 2 dc,
1 dc in each of last 3 dc, turn. *69 (76: 83) dc.***
Cut off A and change to B.
Work straight for 10 rows, ending with a
WS row.
Next row (RS) 1 ss in each of first 8 (9: 10) dc,
1 ch, 1 dc in same place as ss, 1 dc in each dc to
last 7 (8: 9) dc, turn. *55 (60: 65) dc.*
Next row (dec row) 1 ch, 1 dc in first dc, work
dc2tog over next 2 dc, 1 dc in each dc to last
3 dc, work dc2tog over next 2 dc, 1 dc in last
dc, turn.
Work straight for 3 rows, ending with a RS row.
Rep last 4 rows 3 times more and then the dec
row again. *45 (50: 55) dc.*

Work straight until Front measures 43 (48: 53) cm/17 (19: 21) in from beg, ending with a WS row.

Divide for straps
Next row (RS) 1 ch, 1 dc in each of first 9 (11: 13) dc, turn. *9 (11: 13) dc.*
Working on these sts only for first strap, cont as follows:
Work straight until strap measures 32 (34: 40) cm/ 12½ (13½: 15¾) in.
Fasten off.
With RS facing, return to sts left unworked, miss centre 27 (28: 29) dc and rejoin B with a ss to next dc, 1 ch, 1 dc in same place as ss, 1 dc in each dc to end, turn. *9 (11: 13) dc.*
Work straight until strap measures 32 (34: 40) cm/ 12½ (13½: 15¾) in.
Fasten off.

BACK
Work as given for Front to **.
Cut off A and change to B.
Work straight for 4 rows, ending with a WS row.
Work buttonholes over next 2 rows as follows:
Buttonhole row 1 (RS) 1 ch, 1 dc in each of first 19 (21: 23) dc, 4 ch, miss next 4 dc, 1 dc in each dc to last 23 (25: 27) dc, 4 ch, miss next 4 dc, 1 dc in each dc to end, turn.
Buttonhole row 2 1 ch, *1 dc in each dc to 4-ch sp, 4 dc in 4-ch sp; rep from * once, 1 dc in each dc to end, turn.
Work straight for 4 rows.
Fasten off.

POCKETS (make 2)
Using 2.50mm (US size C-2) hook and B, make 19 ch.
Foundation row (RS) 1 dc in 2nd ch from hook, 1 dc in each of rem ch, turn. *18 dc.*
Row 1 (patt row) 1 ch (does NOT count as a st), 1 dc in each dc to end, turn.
(Last row forms simple dc patt when repeated.)
Cont in dc throughout, work 17 rows more, ending with a RS row.

Next row (WS) 3 ch (to count as first tr), miss first dc, 1 tr in each dc to end. *18 sts.*
Fasten off.

Picot pocket trimming
With RS of pocket facing and using 2.50mm (US size C-2) hook and A, working trimming at top of pocket along last dc row as follows:
Row 1 (RS) Insert hook from front to back and through to front again around first 2 dc of last row of dc, yrh and draw a loop through fabric and loop on hook, 4 ch, 1 ss in 4th ch from hook, *insert hook from front to back and to front again around next 2 dc, yrh and draw a loop through fabric and loop on hook, 4 ch, 1 ss in 4th ch from hook; rep from * 7 times more.
Fasten off.

TO FINISH
Press pinafore pieces lightly on wrong side, following instructions on yarn label.
Sew side seams on pinafore.
Sew one button to end of each strap.
Using a blunt-ended yarn needle and A, work two large cross stitches at centre of pocket two rows apart as shown, working each one over 2 dc and two rows.
Sew pockets to front of pinafore as shown.

BELT

TO MAKE BELT
The belt is made in two halves, that are joined together lengthways along the centre.

First half
Using 2.50mm (US size C-2) hook and D, make 175 (182: 189) ch.
Fasten off, leaving a long tail-end of yarn.
Foundation row (RS) Using B, join yarn with a ss to first ch, 1 ch (does NOT count as a st), 1 dc in same place as ss, 1 dc in each of rem ch, turn. *175 (182: 189) dc.*
Fasten off.
Row 1 Using A, join yarn with a ss to first dc, 1 ch (does NOT count as a st), 1 dc in same place as ss, 1 dc in each dc to end.
Fasten off.

Second half

Work second half in same way as first half, but turn work at end of row 1 and do not fasten off A. Place first half behind second half with right sides of strips together and tops of last rows aligned, then still using A, join strips by working a row of dc through both pieces at once.

Fasten off.

Edging at ends

Using long tail-end of D, work a row of dc along each short end.

Fasten off.

BELT CARRIERS (make 3)

Using 2.50mm (US size C-2) hook and A, make 8 ch.

Foundation row (RS) 1 dc in 2nd ch from hook, 1 dc in each of rem ch, turn. 7 dc.

Row 1 1 ch (does NOT count as a st), 1 dc in each dc to end.

Fasten off.

TO FINISH

Press pieces lightly on wrong side, following instructions on yarn label.

Sew buckle to one end of belt.

Sew one belt carrier to each side seam and one to centre back. Thread belt through carriers.

FLOWER MOTIFS

LARGE FLOWERS (make 2)

Using 2.50mm (US size C-2) hook and C, make 4 ch and join with a ss to first ch to form a ring.

Round 1 (RS) Using C, 1 ch, 8 dc in ring, change to D and join with a ss to first dc.

(Do not turn at end of rounds, but work with RS always facing.)

Round 2 Using D, 1 ch, 2 dc in same place as ss, [2 dc in next dc] 7 times, change to C and join with a ss to first dc. 16 dc.

Cut off D and cont with C.

Round 3 1 ch, 2 dc in same place as ss, 1 dc in next dc, [2 dc in next dc, 1 dc in next dc] 7 times, join with a ss to first dc. 24 dc.

Round 4 4 ch, 1 ss in 3rd ch from hook, 1 ss in each of first 2 dc, [4 ch, 1 ss in 3rd ch from hook,

1 ss in each of next 2 dc] 11 times, join with a ss to first of 4-ch. 12 picot petals.

Work a 7.5cm/3in length of chain and fasten off.

SMALL FLOWERS (make 4)

Using 2.50mm (US size C-2) hook and B, make 4 ch and join with a ss to first ch to form a ring.

Round 1 Using B, 1 ch, 9 dc in ring, change to D and join with a ss to first dc.

(Do not turn at end of round, but cont with RS facing.)

Cut off B and cont with D.

Round 2 Using D, 4 ch, 1 ss in 3rd ch from hook, 1 ss in first dc, [4 ch, 1 ss in 3rd ch from hook, 1 ss in next dc] 8 times, join with a ss to first of 4-ch. 9 picot petals.

Work a 7.5cm/3in length of chain and fasten off.

TO FINISH

Do not press flowers.

Sew one large flower and two small flowers to Front above each pocket as shown, securing ends of flower stems inside pockets.

If desired, sew a button to centre of each flower.

POSY HEADSCARF

Perfect for those first days of spring and really simple to make, the Posy Headscarf is guaranteed to keep showers away and to make the sun shine — everyone must have one!

BEFORE YOU BEGIN

SIZES AND MEASUREMENTS

To fit ages (in years)	2–3	3–4	4–5
Finished measurement			
Width at widest	30cm	32cm	33cm
	12in	12½in	13in

YARN

Rowan *4-Ply Soft* (50g/1¾ oz balls) as follows:

A	pink (Fairy 395)	1 ball	1 ball	1 ball
B	red (Honk 374)	1 ball	1 ball	1 ball
C	sage green (Leafy 367)	1 ball	1 ball	1 ball
D	pale blue (Whisper 370)	1 ball	1 ball	1 ball

HOOK

2.50mm (US size C-2) crochet hook

TENSION

25 sts and 26 rows to 10cm/4in measured over dc using 2.50mm (US size C-2) crochet hook *or size necessary to obtain correct tension.*

ABBREVIATIONS

dc2tog = [insert hook in next st, yrh and draw a loop through] twice, yrh and draw through all 3 loops on hook — *one st decreased.*

dc3tog = [insert hook in next st, yrh and draw a loop through] 3 times, yrh and draw through all 4 loops on hook — *2 sts decreased.*

See also page 110.

GETTING STARTED

TO MAKE HEADSCARF

Using 2.50mm (US size C-2) hook and B, make 75 (79: 83) ch.
Fasten off.
Change to A on next row as follows:
Foundation row (RS) Join A with a ss to first ch, 1 ch (does NOT count as a st), 1 dc in same place as ss, 1 dc in each of rem ch, turn. *75 (79: 83) dc.*

Row 1 (patt row) 1 ch (does NOT count as a st), 1 dc in each dc to end, turn.
(Last row forms simple dc patt when repeated.)

Row 2 (eyelet row) 4 ch (to count as first tr and first 1-ch sp), miss first 2 dc, 1 tr in next dc, *1 ch, miss 1 dc, 1 tr in next dc; rep from * to end.

Row 3 1 ch, 1 dc in first tr, *1 dc in next 1-ch sp, 1 dc in next tr; rep from * to last 1-ch sp, 1 dc in next 1-ch sp, 1 dc in 3rd of 4-ch, turn. *75 (79: 83) dc.*

Cont in dc throughout, work 2 rows.

Next row (dec row) (RS) 1 ch, 1 dc in first dc, work dc2tog over next 2 dc, 1 dc in each dc to last 3 dc, work dc2tog over next 2 dc, 1 dc in last dc, turn.

Work straight for 1 row.
Rep last 2 rows until 5 dc rem, ending with a WS row.

Next row (RS) 1 ch, 1 dc in first dc, work dc3tog over next 3 dc, 1 dc in last dc, turn. *3 dc.*

Work straight for 1 row.

Next row 1 ch, work dc3tog over 3 dc. *1 dc.*
Fasten off.

LARGE FLOWERS (make 4)

Using 2.50mm (US size C-2) hook and C, make 4 ch and join with a ss to first ch to form a ring.

Round 1 (RS) Using C, 1 ch, 8 dc in ring, change to D and join with a ss to first dc.
(Do not turn at end of rounds, but work with RS always facing.)

Round 2 Using D, 1 ch, 2 dc same place as ss, [2 dc in next dc] 7 times, change to C and join with a ss to first dc. *16 dc.*
Cut off D and cont with C.

Round 3 1 ch, 2 dc in same place as ss, 1 dc in next dc, [2 dc in next dc, 1 dc in next dc] 7 times, join with a ss to first dc. *24 dc.*

Round 4 4 ch, 1 ss in 3rd ch from hook, 1 ss in each of first 2 dc, [4 ch, 1 ss in 3rd ch from hook, 1 ss in each of next 2 dc] 11 times, join with a ss

to first of 4-ch. *12 picot petals.*
Fasten off.

SMALL FLOWERS (make 6)

Using 2.50mm (US size C-2) hook and B, make
4 ch and join with a ss to first ch to form a ring.
Round 1 Using B, 1 ch, 9 dc in ring, change to D
and join with a ss to first dc.
(Do not turn at end of round, but cont with RS
facing.)
Cut off B and cont with D.
Round 2 4 ch, 1 ss in 3rd ch from hook, 1 ss in
first dc, [4 ch, 1 ss in 3rd ch from hook, 1 ss in
next dc] 8 times, join with a ss to first of 4-ch.
9 picot petals.
Fasten off.

TIE

Make a twisted cord for tie as follows:
Cut two strands of B, each approximately
2.5m/2¾yd long. Align the strands and knot them
together at each end. Hook one end over a
door handle, and insert a pencil through the
other end. Twist pencil clockwise until strands
are tightly twisted. Holding cord in centre with
one hand, bring ends together and let two
halves twist together.
Knot each end to make a finished cord
79cm/31in long. Trim ends 1cm/¼in from knots.

TO FINISH

Do not press flowers.
Press headscarf lightly on wrong side, following
instructions on yarn label.
Sew flowers to right side of headscarf in
random positions.
Thread tie through eyelet row.

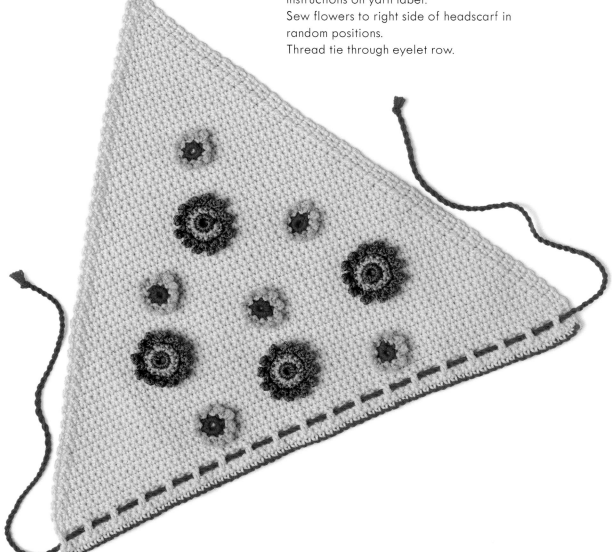

MARCEL THE SNAIL TOP

Snails are always out and about in the spring, and Marcel is no exception. Simple stripes and running-stitch detail make this little top extra special. As it is so easily made in double crochet, you can be outside wearing it with the snails in no time!

BEFORE YOU BEGIN

SIZES AND MEASUREMENTS

To fit ages (in years)	2–3	3–4	4–5
To fit chest	56cm	61cm	66cm
	22in	24in	26in
Finished measurements			
Around chest	68cm	74cm	79cm
	26¾in	29in	31in
Length to shoulder	28cm	30cm	32cm
	11in	11¾in	12½in

YARN

Rowan *4-Ply Soft* (50g/1¾ oz balls) as follows:

		2–3	3–4	4–5
A	charcoal (Sooty 372)	2 balls	2 balls	3 balls
B	pale blue (Whisper 370)	1 ball	2 balls	2 balls
C	sage green (Leafy 367)	1 ball	1 ball	1 ball
D	ecru (Linseed 393)	1 ball	1 ball	1 ball

HOOK

2.50mm (US size C-2) crochet hook

EXTRAS

2 red buttons 11mm/⁷⁄₁₆in in diameter, for snail motif (snail is optional)

TENSION

25 sts and 26 rows to 10cm/4in measured over dc using 2.50mm (US size C-2) crochet hook *or size necessary to obtain correct tension.*

ABBREVIATIONS

dc2tog = [insert hook in next st, yrh and draw a loop through] twice, yrh and draw through all 3 loops on hook – *one st decreased.*
See also page 110.

GETTING STARTED

TOP

BACK

Using 2.50mm (US size C-2) hook and C, make 85 (92: 99) ch.
Fasten off.
Change to A on next row as follows:
Foundation row (RS) Join A with a ss to first ch, 1 ch (does NOT count as a st), 1 dc in same place as ss, 1 dc in each of rem ch, turn. *85 (92: 99) dc.*
Row 1 (patt row) 1 ch (does NOT count as a st), 1 dc in each dc to end, turn.
(Last row forms simple dc patt when repeated.)
Cont in dc throughout, work in stripe sequence of [2 rows B, 2 rows A] repeated until Back measures 13 (14: 15) cm/5¼ (5½: 6) in from beg, ending with a WS row.
Cut off B.
Cont in A only, work until Back measures 16 (17: 18) cm/6¼ (6¾: 7) in from beg, ending with a WS row.

Shape armholes

Next row (RS) 1 ss in each of first 8 (9: 10) dc, 1 ch, 1 dc in same place as last ss, 1 dc in each dc to last 7 (8: 9) dc, turn. *71 (76: 81) dc.*
Next row 1 ch, 1 dc in first dc, work dc2tog over next 2 dc, 1 dc in each dc to last 3 dc, work dc2tog over next 2 dc, 1 dc in last dc, turn.
Rep last row 4 times more. *61 (66: 71) dc.***
Work straight until Back measures 26 (28: 30) cm/10¼ (11: 11¾) in from beg, ending with a WS row.

Shape back neck

Next row (RS) 1 ch, 1 dc in each of first 12 (13: 14) dc, work dc2tog over next 2 dc, 1 dc in next dc, turn. *14 (15: 16) dc.*
Working on these sts only for first side of neck, cont as follows:
Next row 1 ch, 1 dc in first dc, work dc2tog over next 2 dc, 1 dc in each dc to end, turn. *13 (14: 15) dc.*

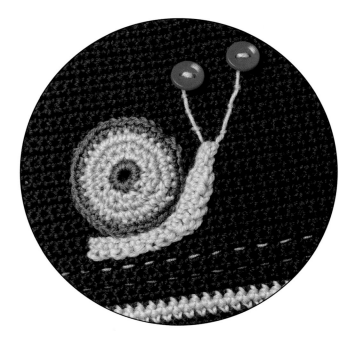

Next row 1 ch, 1 dc in each dc to last 3 dc, work dc2tog over next 2 dc, 1 dc in last dc, turn. *12 (13: 14) dc.*
Dec 1 st at neck edge on each of next 3 rows, working decreases as set. *9 (10: 11) dc.*
Fasten off.
With RS facing, return to sts left unworked, miss centre 31 (34: 37) dc and rejoin A with a ss to next dc, 1 ch, 1 dc in same place as ss, work dc2tog over next 2 dc, 1 dc in each dc to end, turn. *14 (15: 16) dc.*
Next row 1 ch, 1 dc in each dc to last 3 dc, work dc2tog over next 2 dc, 1 dc in last dc, turn. *13 (14: 15) dc.*
Next row 1 ch, 1 dc in first dc, work dc2tog over next 2 dc, 1 dc in each dc to end, turn. *12 (13: 14) dc.*
Dec 1 st at neck edge on each of next 3 rows, working decreases as set. *9 (10: 11) dc.*
Fasten off.

FRONT
Work as for Back to **.
Work straight until 20 rows less have been worked than Back to fasten-off at shoulder, ending with a WS row.

Shape front neck
Next row RS) 1 ch, 1 dc in each of first 16 (17: 18) dc, work dc2tog over next 2 dc, 1 dc in next dc, turn. *18 (19: 20) dc.*
Working on these sts only for first side of neck, cont as follows:
Next row 1 ch, 1 dc in each dc to end, turn.
Next row 1 ch, 1 dc in each dc to last 3 dc, work dc2tog over next 2 dc, 1 dc in last dc, turn.
Rep last 2 rows until 9 (10: 11) dc rem.
Work straight for 1 row.
Fasten off.
With RS facing, return to sts left unworked, miss centre 23 (26: 29) dc and rejoin A with a ss to next dc, 1 ch, 1 dc in same place as ss, work dc2tog over next 2 dc, 1 dc in each to end, turn.
Next row 1 ch, 1 dc in each dc to end, turn.
Next row 1 ch, 1 dc in first dc, work dc2tog over next 2 dc, 1 dc in each dc to end, turn.
Rep last 2 rows until 9 (10: 11) dc rem.
Work straight for 1 row.
Fasten off.

TO FINISH
Press pieces lightly on wrong side, following instructions on yarn label.
Sew shoulder seams.

Neck edging
With RS facing and using 2.50mm (US size C-2) hook and B, work edging along neck as follows:
Round 1 (RS) Join B with a ss to neck edge at left shoulder seam, 1 ch, 1 dc in same place as ss, then work a round of dc evenly around neck edge, join with a ss to first dc.
Fasten off.
With RS facing, join in D on next round as follows:
Round 2 (RS) Join D with a ss to first dc at beg of last round, 1 ch, 1 dc in same place as ss, 1 dc in each dc to end of round, join with a ss to first dc.
Fasten off.
With RS facing, join in C on next round as follows:
Round 3 (RS) Join C with a ss to first dc at beg of last round, 1 ch, 1 dc

in each dc to 1 dc before first of 2 corners on centre front neck, work dc2tog over next 2 dc (to shape corner), 1 dc in each dc to 1 dc before second corner, work dc2tog over next 2 dc, 1 dc in each dc to end of round, join with a ss to first dc.
Fasten off.

Armhole edgings (both alike)
Sew side seams.
With RS facing and using 2.50mm (US size C-2) hook and B, work edging around each armhole edge as follows:
Round 1 (RS) Join B with a ss to armhole edge at side seam, 1 ch, 1 dc in same place as ss, then work a round of dc evenly around armhole edge, join with a ss to first dc.
Fasten off.
With RS facing, join in D on next round as follows:
Round 2 (RS) Join D with a ss to first dc at beg of last round, 1 ch, 1 dc in same place as ss, 1 dc in each dc to end of round, join with a ss to first dc.
Fasten off.
With RS facing, join in C and work next round as for round 2. Fasten off.

Embroidery
Using a blunt-ended yarn needle, work embroidery on top as follows:
Using C, work running stitches all around the top, between the third and fourth row in A above the last stripe in B; work the running stitches over one dc and under one dc alternately.
Using D, work a second line of running stitches in the same way all around the top, two rows above first line of running stitches.

SNAIL MOTIF (optional)
SNAIL'S SHELL Ⓐ
Using 2.50mm (US size C-2) hook and C, make 4 ch and join with a ss to first ch to form a ring.
Round 1 (RS) 1 ch, 8 dc in ring, change to B and join with a ss to first dc. *8 dc.*
(Do not turn at end of rounds, but work with RS always facing.)

Round 2 Using B, 1 ch, 2 dc in each dc to end of round, change to D and join with a ss to first dc. *16 dc.*
Round 3 Using D, 1 ch, [2 dc in next dc, 1 dc in next dc] 8 times, change to B and join with a ss to first dc. *24 dc.*
Round 4 Using B, 1 ch, [2 dc in next dc, 1 dc in each of next 2 dc] 8 times, change to C and join with a ss to first dc. *32 dc.*
Round 5 Using C, 1 ch, [2 dc in next dc, 1 dc in each of next 3 dc] 8 times, join with a ss to first dc. *40 dc.*
Fasten off.

SNAIL'S BODY Ⓑ
Using 2.50mm (US size C-2) hook and B, make 18 ch.
Foundation row (RS) 1 ss in 2nd ch from hook, 1 ss in next ch, 1 dc in next ch, 1 htr in each of next 2 ch, 1 tr in each of next 3 ch, 1 htr in next ch, 1 dc in next ch, 1 ss in each of next 2 ch, 1 dc in each of last 5 ch.
Fasten off.

TO FINISH
Sew snail's shell and body to front just above top line of running stitches and under right shoulder, positioning top of foundation row of body along belly of snail as shown.
Using a blunt-ended yarn needle and B, work a couched line for each of the snail's antenna as shown. Sew a button to top of each antenna.

LITTLE STRIPY BAG

Very simple and very stylish, this Little Stripy Bag is useful for keeping all your favourite things in. Make the strap long enough to go over your head or short to use as a handbag — whatever suits you!

BEFORE YOU BEGIN

SIZE
The finished bag measures approximately 17cm/6¾in wide by 17cm/6¾in deep.

YARN
Rowan *4-Ply Soft* (50g/1¾oz balls) as follows:

A sage green (Leafy 367)		1 ball
B pale blue (Whisper 370)		1 ball
C red (Honk 374)		1 ball

HOOK
2.50mm (US size C-2) crochet hook

TENSION
25 sts and 26 rows to 10cm/4in measured over dc using 2.50mm (US size C-2) crochet hook or *size necessary to obtain correct tension.*

ABBREVIATIONS
See page 110.

GETTING STARTED

MAIN SECTION OF BAG
The main section of the bag is worked in one piece that is folded in half to form the bag.
Using 2.50mm (US size C-2) hook and A, make 69 ch.
Foundation row (RS) 1 dc in 2nd ch from hook, 1 dc in each of rem ch, turn. 68 *dc.*
Row 1 (patt row) 1 ch (does NOT count as a st), 1 dc in each dc to end, turn.
(Last row forms simple dc patt when repeated.)
Cont in dc throughout, **work 2 rows B, 2 rows A, 2 rows C and 2 rows A.**
Rep from ** to ** 4 times more (a total of 42 rows worked from beg).
Work 2 rows B, 2 rows A (a total of 46 rows worked from beg).
Fasten off.

TO FINISH
Press main section of bag lightly on wrong side, following instructions on yarn label.

Top borders (both alike)
With RS facing and using 2.50mm (US size C-2) hook and A, work top border along each side-edge of main section as follows:
Row 1 (RS) Join A with a ss to first row-end, 1 ch (does NOT count as a st), 1 dc in same place as ss, *1 dc in each of rem row-ends, turn. 46 *dc.*
Row 2 1 ch, 1 dc in each dc to end, turn.
Rep last row 5 times more, ending with a RS row.
Fasten off.
Fold main section in half widthways with right sides together and sew side seams. Turn right side out.

Edging
With RS facing and using 2.50mm (US size C-2) hook and C, work edging along top of bag as follows:
Round 1 (RS) Join C with a ss to a dc at side seam, 2 ch (to count as first dc and first 1-ch sp), miss next dc, *1 dc in next dc, 1 ch, miss next dc; rep from * all around top of bag, join with a ss to first of 2-ch.
Fasten off.
With RS facing, join in B on next round as follows:
Round 2 (RS) Join B with a ss to last 1-ch sp of last round, 2 ch (to count as first dc and first 1-ch sp), *1 dc in next 1-ch sp, 1 ch; rep from * end of round, join with a ss to first of 2-ch.
Fasten off.
With RS facing, join in A and work next round as for round 2.
Fasten off.

Bag strap
Make a twisted cord for bag strap as follows:

Cut four strands of A, each approximately 3m/3¼yd long. Align the strands and knot them together at each end. Hook one end over a door handle, and insert a pencil through the other end. Twist pencil clockwise until strands are tightly twisted. Holding cord in centre with one hand, bring ends together and let two halves twist together.

Knot each end to make a finished strap 108cm/42½in long. Trim ends close to knots. Starting at one corner at bottom edge of bag, sew ends of cord to inside of bag all along side seams.

BON-BON BLANKET

This very special little Bon-Bon Blanket with its dainty circles in candy stripes is surprisingly easy to make – all you need to do is work simple rounds of treble crochet. Once it's made, enjoy it all the more by sharing it with a friend.

SIZE
The finished blanket measures approximately 93cm/36½in wide by 117cm/46in long, including the edging.
Note: To make a smaller or bigger blanket, simply make fewer or more circles.

YARN
Rowan *4-Ply Soft* (50g/1¾oz balls) as follows:

A	pink (Fairy 395)	7 balls
B	red (Honk 374)	6 balls
C	sage green (Leafy 367)	2 balls
D	sea green (Folly 391)	2 balls

HOOK
2.50mm (US size C-2) crochet hook

TENSION
Each large circle measures 6cm/2⅜in in diameter using a 2.50mm (US size C-2) crochet hook *or whatever size necessary to obtain correct tension.*

ABBREVIATIONS
dc2tog = [insert hook in next st, yrh and draw a loop through] twice, yrh and draw through all 3 loops on hook – *one st decreased.*
See also page 110.

LARGE CIRCLE 1 (make 143)
Using 2.50mm (US size C-2) hook and A, make 6 ch and join with a ss to first ch to form a ring.
Round 1 (RS) Using A, 3 ch (to count as first tr), 15 tr in ring, change to B and join with a ss to 3rd of 3-ch. *16 sts.*
(Do not turn at end of rounds, but work with RS always facing.)
Round 2 Using B, 3 ch, 1 tr in same place as last ss, 2 tr in each tr to end of round, change to A and join with a ss to 3rd of 3-ch. *32 sts.*
Cut off B.
Round 3 Using A, 3 ch, 1 tr in same place as last ss, 1 tr in next tr, *2 tr in next tr, 1 tr in next tr; rep from * to end of round, join with a ss in 3rd of 3-ch. *48 sts.*
Fasten off, leaving a long tail-end of yarn.

LARGE CIRCLE 2 (make 142)
Work as for Large Circle 1, but use B in place of A, and A in place of B.

SMALL CIRCLE 1 (make 126)
Using 2.50mm (US size C-2) hook and C, make 6 ch and join with a ss to first ch to form a ring.
Round 1 (RS) 3 ch (to count as first tr), 15 tr in ring, join with a ss to 3rd of 3-ch. *16 sts.*
Fasten off, leaving a long tail-end of yarn.

SMALL CIRCLE 2 (make 126)
Work as for Small Circle 1, but use D instead of C.

TO FINISH
Arrange all large circles in a rectangle 15 circles wide by 19 circles long, with a Large Circle 1 at each of four corners and alternating Large Circles 1 and 2 (see below).
Using long tail-ends of yarn, sew together large

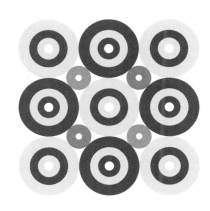

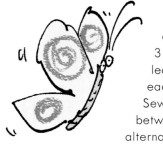

circles by stitching together 3 tr where circles touch (and leaving 9 tr free between each 3-tr joining point). Sew small circles into spaces between large circles, alternating Small Circles 1 and 2.

Edging

With RS facing and using 2.50mm (US size C-2) hook, work edging around blanket as follows:

Round 1 (RS) Using D, join yarn with a ss to a corner tr, 1 ch (does NOT count as a st), 1 dc in same place as ss, *1 dc in each tr to 1 tr before 3-tr joining point, work dc2tog over next tr and first free tr on next circle; rep from * all around edge of blanket, 1 dc in each tr to end of round, join with a ss to first dc.
Fasten off.
(Do not turn at end of rounds, but work with RS always facing.)

Round 2 Using C, join yarn with a ss to same place as last ss, 1 ch, 1 dc in same place as ss, *1 dc in each dc to 1 dc before dc2tog, then insert hook in next dc, yrh and draw a loop through, miss next st (which is top of dc2tog) and insert hook in next dc, yrh and draw a loop through, yrh and draw through all 3 loops on hook to complete dc2tog; rep from * all around, 1 dc in each dc to end of round, join with a ss to first dc.
Fasten off.

Round 3 Using A, rep round 2.
Fasten off.

Round 4 Using B, rep round 2.
Fasten off.

Round 5 Using A, join yarn with a ss to same place as last ss, 1 ch, 1 dc in same place as ss, 1 dc in each dc to end.
Fasten off.

Press lightly on wrong side, following instructions on yarn label.

SWEET CICELY SKIRT

This gorgeous skirt is easily made in a simple textured stitch. It is Sweet Cicely's favourite and is really comfortable to wear with pretty pockets, edgings and buttons. When worn with the Sweet Cicely Top (see page 34), it makes a fantastic outfit. The Summer Cap and Best Beach Bag (see pages 38 and 49) complement it perfectly. Sweet Cicely really does look very sweet, doesn't she!

SIZES AND MEASUREMENTS

To fit ages (in years)	2–3	3–4	4–5
Finished measurements			
Length to waist	26cm	31cm	36cm
	10¼ in	12¼ in	14¼ in

YARN

Rowan *4-Ply Cotton* (50g/1¾ oz balls) as follows:

A pale green (Fresh 131)	3 balls	4 balls	4 balls
B mid green (Fennel 135)	1 ball	1 ball	1 ball

Rowan *Cotton Glace* (50g/1¾ oz balls) as follows:

C red (Poppy 741)	1 ball	1 ball	1 ball

HOOKS

2.50mm (US size C-2) crochet hook
3.00mm (US size D-3) crochet hook

EXTRAS

2 red buttons 18mm/¾ in in diameter, for pocket flaps

TENSION

30 sts and 18 rows to 10cm/4in measured over patt using A and 3.00mm (US size D-3) crochet hook *or size necessary to obtain correct tension*.

ABBREVIATIONS

dc2tog = [insert hook in next st, yrh and draw a loop through] twice, yrh and draw through all 3 loops on hook – *one st decreased*.
See also page 110.

FRONT OF SKIRT

Using 3.00mm (US size D-3) hook and A, make 131 (145: 163) ch.

Foundation row (RS) 1 dc and 1 htr in 3rd ch from hook, *miss next ch, 1 dc and 1 htr in next ch; rep from * to end, turn. *130 (144: 162) sts.*

Row 1 (patt row) 2 ch (does NOT count as a st), 1 dc and 1 htr in first htr, *1 dc and 1 htr in next htr; rep from * to end, turn.
(Last row forms patt when repeated.)
Work 0 (2: 6) rows more in patt, ending with a WS row.

Next row (dec row) (RS) 2 ch, 1 dc and 1 htr in first htr, [1 dc and 1 htr in next htr] 9 times, 1 dc in next htr, 1 htr in next htr, work in patt to last 24 sts, 1 dc in next htr, 1 htr in next htr, [1 dc and 1 htr in next htr] 10 times, turn. *(4 sts decreased.)*
Work straight in patt for 3 rows.
Rep last 4 rows 8 (9: 11) times more and then the dec row again. *90 (100: 110) sts.*
Work straight in patt until Front measures 24 (29: 34) cm/9½ (11½ : 13½) in from beg, ending with a RS row.

Next row (WS) 1 ch (does NOT count as a st), 1 dc in each st to end, turn. *90 (100: 110) dc.*
Cut off A.

Waistband

Change to 2.50mm (US size C-2) hook and B and work waistband as follows:

Next row (dec row) (RS) 1 ch, 1 dc in each of first 2 (7: 12) dc, work dc2tog over next 2 dc, [1 dc in next dc, work dc2tog over next 2 dc] 28 times, 1 dc in each of last 2 (7: 12) dc, turn. *61 (71: 81) dc.*

Next row 1 ch, 1 dc in each dc to end, turn.
Rep last row twice more.

Next row (eyelet row) (RS) 1 ch, 1 dc in each of first 2 dc, *3 ch, miss next 2 dc, 1 dc in each of next 3 dc; rep from * to last 4 dc, 3 ch, miss next 2 dc, 1 dc in each of last 2 dc, turn.

Next row 1 ch, 1 dc in each of first 2 dc, *2 dc in next 3-ch sp, 1 dc in each of next 3 dc; rep from

* to last 3-ch sp, 2 dc in next 3-ch sp, 1 dc in each of last 2 dc, turn.

Next row 1 ch, 1 dc in each dc to end.
Fasten off.

BACK OF SKIRT

Work exactly as for Front of Skirt.

POCKETS (make 2)

Using 3.00mm (US size D-3) hook and A, make 23 ch.

Foundation row (RS) 1 dc and 1 htr in 3rd ch from hook, *miss next ch, 1 dc and 1 htr in next ch; rep from * to end, turn. 22 *sts.*

Row 1 (patt row) 2 ch (does NOT count as a st), 1 dc and 1 htr in first htr, *1 dc and 1 htr in next htr; rep from * to end, turn.
(Last row forms patt when repeated.)
Work straight in patt for 12 rows, ending with a WS row.

Pocket flap

Next row (RS of pocket, WS of flap) 1 ch (does NOT count as a st), 1 dc in each st to end, turn. 22 *dc.*

Next row (dec row) 1 ch, 1 dc in first dc, work dc2tog over next 2 dc, 1 dc in each dc to last 3 dc, work dc2tog over next 2 dc, 1 dc in last dc, turn.
Rep last row 7 times more. 6 *dc.*

Next row 1 ch, 1 dc in first dc, [work dc2tog over next 2 dc] twice, 1 dc in last dc, turn. 4 *dc.*

Next row 1 ch, [work dc2tog over next 2 dc] twice. 2 *dc.*
Fasten off.

Pocket edging

With RS of pocket flap (and WS of pocket) facing and using 2.50mm (US size C-2) hook and B, work edging along edge of shaped pocket flap as follows:

Row 1 (RS) Join B with a ss to first row-end at beg of side-edge of flap, 1 ch, 1 dc in same place as ss, miss next row-end, [3 tr and 1 ss in next row-end, 1 dc in next row-end, miss next row-end] 3 times, 3 tr and 1 ss in centre of top of last row of flap, then cont along other side of flap and miss first row-end, [1 dc in next row-end, 3 tr and 1 ss in next row-end, miss next

row-end] 3 times 1 dc in last row-end.
Fasten off.

TO FINISH

Press pieces lightly on wrong side, following instructions on yarn label.
Fold each pocket flap to right side of pocket and secure in place with a button. Sew pockets to Front of Skirt as shown on opposite page.
Sew Front and Back of skirt together along side edges.

Skirt-hem edging

With RS facing and using 2.50mm (US size C-2) hook and B, work edging along foundation-chain edge of skirt as follows:

Round 1 (RS) Join B with a ss to 1-ch sp at a side seam, 1 ch, 1 dc in same place as ss, *3 tr and 1 ss in next ch sp, 1 dc in next ch sp; rep from * to last ch sp, 3 tr in last ch sp, join with a ss to first dc.
Fasten off.

Drawstring

Using 2.50mm (US size C-2) hook and C and leaving a long tail-end (about 100cm/39½in long), make a ch long enough to fit around waist and tie neatly (approximately 72cm/28½in long), then work 10 tr in 3rd ch from hook to form a bobble at end of chain.
Fasten off, thread this tail-end of yarn through top of tr, pull up tightly to complete bobble and secure.
Beginning at centre front of skirt, thread drawstring chain through eyelet holes in waistband. Then work a bobble in same way as first bobble at other end of drawstring, using the long tail-end at beginning of foundation chain.

33

SWEET CICELY TOP

The Sweet Cicely Top is just the thing to wear on a warm summer's day at the beach. It is easily made in simple double and half treble crochet. The cotton yarn will keep you cool and the lovely little cap sleeves will keep the sun off delicate shoulders. Slip it on and have a good splash about.

BEFORE YOU BEGIN

SIZES AND MEASUREMENTS

To fit ages (in years)	2–3	3–4	4–5
To fit chest	56cm	61cm	66cm
	22in	24in	26in
Finished measurements			
Around chest	69cm	75cm	80cm
	27in	29½in	31½in
Length to shoulder	30cm	32cm	34cm
	11¾in	12½in	13½in

YARN

Rowan *4-Ply Cotton* (50g/1¾ oz balls) as follows:			
A mid green (Fennel 135)	2 balls	3 balls	3 balls
B pale green (Fresh 131)	1 ball	1 ball	1 ball
Rowan *Cotton Glace* (50g/1¾ oz balls) as follows:			
C red (Poppy 741)	1 ball	1 ball	1 ball

HOOKS

2.50mm (US size C-2) crochet hook
3.00mm (US size D-3) crochet hook

TENSION

23 htr and 18 rows to 10cm/4in measured over htr using A and 3.00mm (US size D-3) crochet hook *or size necessary to obtain correct tension.*
23 dc and 26 rows to 10cm/4in measured over dc using A and 3.00mm (US size D-3) crochet hook *or size necessary to obtain correct tension.*

ABBREVIATIONS

dc2tog = [insert hook in next st, yrh and draw a loop through] twice, yrh and draw through all 3 loops on hook — *one st decreased.*
htr2tog = [yrh and insert hook in next st, yrh and draw a loop through] twice, yrh and draw through all 5 loops on hook — *one st decreased.* See also page 110.

GETTING STARTED

BACK

Using 3.00mm (US size D-3) hook and A, make 91 (97: 103) ch.
Foundation row (RS) 1 htr in 3rd ch from hook, 1 htr in each of rem ch, turn. 90 *(96: 102) sts.*
Row 1 (patt row) 2 ch (to count as first htr), miss first htr, 1 htr in each htr to end, 1 htr in 2nd of 2-ch, turn.
(Last row forms simple htr patt when repeated.)
Cont in htr, work 2 rows more in A and 2 rows in B, ending with a WS row.
Next row (dec row) (RS) Using A, 2 ch, miss first htr, 1 tr in each of next 4 htr, work htr2tog over next 2 htr, 1 htr in each htr to last 6 htr, work htr2tog over next 2 htr, 1 tr in each of next 4 htr, 1 htr in 2nd of 2-ch, turn.
Cont in htr, work 1 row more in A and 2 rows in B.
Rep last 4 rows 4 times more, ending with a WS row. 80 *(86: 92) sts.*
Cut off B and cont in A only.
Next row (RS) 1 ch (does NOT count as a st), 1 dc in first htr, 1 dc in each htr to end, 1 dc in 2nd of 2-ch, turn. 80 *(86: 92) dc.*
Next row 1 ch, 1 dc in each dc to end, turn.
Rep last row until Back measures 17 (18: 19) cm/ 6¾ (7: 7½) in from beg, ending with a RS row.

Shape armholes

Next row (WS) 1 ss in each of first 5 dc, 1 ch, 1 dc in same dc as last ss, 1 dc in each dc to last 4 dc, turn. 72 *(78: 84) dc.***
Next row 1 ch, 1 dc in first dc, work dc2tog over next 2 dc, 1 dc in each dc to last 3 dc, work dc2tog over next 2 dc, 1 dc in last dc, turn.
Rep last row 19 (21: 23) times more, ending with a WS row. 32 *(34: 36) dc.*
Fasten off.

FRONT

Work as for Back to **.

Next row (RS) 1 ch, 1 dc in first dc, work dc2tog over next 2 dc, 1 dc in each dc to last 3 dc, work dc2tog over next 2 dc, 1 dc in last dc, turn.
Rep last row 9 (11: 13) times more, ending with a WS row. *52 (54: 56) dc.*

Divide for front neck opening

Next row (RS) 1 ch, 1 dc in first dc, work dc2tog over next 2 dc, 1 dc in each of next 23 (24: 25) dc, turn. *25 (26: 27) dc.*
Working on these sts only for first side of neck opening, cont as follows:

Next row 1 ch, 1 dc in each dc to last 3 dc, work dc2tog over next 2 dc, 1 dc in last dc, turn.
Next row 1 ch, 1 dc in first dc, work dc2tog over next 2 dc, 1 dc in each dc to end, turn.
Next row 1 ch, 1 dc in each dc to last 3 dc, work dc2tog over next 2 dc, 1 dc in last dc, turn.
Rep last 2 rows 3 times more, ending with a WS row. *16 (17: 18) dc.*
Fasten off.

With RS facing, return to sts left unworked and rejoin A with a ss to next dc, 1 ch, 1 dc in same dc as ss, 1 dc in each dc to last 3 dc, work dc2tog over next 2 dc, 1 dc in last dc, turn.
Next row 1 ch, 1 dc in first dc, work dc2tog over next 2 dc, 1 dc in each dc to end, turn.
Next row 1 ch, 1 dc in each dc to last 3 dc, work dc2tog over next 2 dc, 1 dc in last dc, turn.
Next row 1 ch, 1 dc in first dc, work dc2tog over next 2 dc, 1 dc in each dc to end, turn.
Rep last 2 rows 3 times more, ending with a WS row. *16 (17: 18) dc.*
Do NOT fasten off, but leave this ball of A at neck edge to work neck edging later.

SLEEVES (make 2)

Using 3.00mm (US size D-3) hook and A, make 66 (71: 76) ch.
Foundation row (RS) 1 dc in 2nd ch from hook, 1 dc in each of rem ch, turn. *65 (70: 75) dc.*
Row 1 (patt row) 1 ch (does NOT count as a st), 1 dc in each dc to end, turn.
(Last row forms simple dc patt when repeated.)
Next row (inc row) 1 ch, 1 dc in each of first 3 dc, 2 dc in next dc, 1 dc in each dc to last 4 dc,

2 dc in next dc, 1 dc in each of last 3 dc, turn.
Cont in dc throughout, work straight for 2 rows.
Rep last 3 rows 0 (1: 2) times more. *67 (74: 81) dc.*
Next row (inc row) 1 ch, 1 dc in each of first 3 dc, 2 dc in next dc, 1 dc in each dc to last 4 dc, 2 dc in next dc, 1 dc in each of last 3 dc, turn. *69 (76: 83) dc.*
Work straight for 3 (2: 1) rows.

Shape top of sleeve

Next row 1 ss in each of first 5 dc, 1 ch, 1 dc in same dc as last ss, 1 dc in each dc to last 4 dc, turn. *61 (68: 75) dc.*
Next row 1 ch, 1 dc in first dc, work dc2tog over next 2 dc, 1 dc in each dc to last 3 dc, work dc2tog over next 2 dc, 1 dc in last dc, turn.
Rep last row 19 (21: 23) times more. *21 (24: 27) dc.*
Fasten off.

TO FINISH

Press pieces lightly on wrong side, following instructions on yarn label.
Sew sleeves to Back and Front along raglan edges.

Neck edging

With RS facing and using 3.00mm (US size D-3) hook, pick up A left at beg of neck edge on right front and cont as follows:
Row 1 (RS) 1 ch, 1 dc in each of first 15 (16: 17) dc, work dc2tog over last dc of front neck edge and first dc of right sleeve neck edge, 1 dc in each of next 19 (22: 25) dc, work dc2tog over last dc of sleeve neck edge and first dc of back neck edge, 1 dc in each of next 14 (15: 16) dc, work dc2tog over next 2 dc, 1 dc in each of next 14 (15: 16) dc, work dc2tog over last dc of back neck edge and first dc of left sleeve neck edge, 1 dc in each of next 19 (22: 25) dc, work dc2tog over last dc of sleeve neck edge and first dc of left front neck edge, 1 dc in each dc to end, turn. *101 (111: 121) dc.*
Row 2 1 ch, 1 dc in each dc to end, turn.
Row 3 (eyelet row) 1 ch, 1 dc in each of first 2 dc, *3 ch, miss next 2 dc, 1 dc in each of next 3 dc; rep from * to last 4 dc, 3 ch, miss next 2 dc,

1 dc in each of last 2 dc, turn.

Row 4 1 ch, 1 dc in each of first 2 dc, *2 dc in next 3-ch sp, 1 dc in each of next 3 dc; rep from * to last 3-ch sp, 2 dc in next 3-ch sp, 1 dc in each of next 2 dc, turn.

Row 5 1 ch, 1 dc in each dc to end.
Fasten off.

Hem edging

Sew side and sleeve seams.

With RS facing and using 2.50mm (US size C-2) hook and A, work edging along foundation-chain edge of top as follows:

Round 1 (RS) Join A with a ss to first ch of foundation-chain edge of top at a side seam, 1 dc in same place as ss, *miss 1 ch, [3 tr, 1 ss] both in next ch, miss 1 ch, 1 dc in next ch; rep from * to last 3 ch, miss 1 ch, [3 tr, 1 ss] both in next ch, join with a ss to first dc.
Fasten off.

Sleeve edging

With RS facing and using 2.50mm (US size C-2) hook and A, work edging along edge of sleeve as follows:

Round 1 (RS) Join A with a ss to first ch of foundation-chain edge of sleeve at side seam, 1 dc in same place as ss, *miss 2 ch, [3 tr, 1 ss] both in next ch, miss 1 ch, 1 dc in next ch; rep from * to last 3 ch, miss 1 ch, [3 tr, 1 ss] both in next ch, join with a ss to first dc.
Fasten off.

Drawstring

Using 2.50mm (US size C-2) hook and C and leaving a long tail-end (about 100cm/39½in long), make a ch long enough to fit around neck and tie neatly (approximately 56cm/22in long), then work 10 tr in 3rd ch from hook to form a bobble at end of chain. Fasten off, thread this tail-end of yarn through top of tr, pull up tightly to complete bobble and secure.

Beginning at centre front neck opening, thread drawstring chain through eyelet holes in neck edging. Then work a bobble in same way as first bobble at other end of drawstring, using the long tail-end at beginning of foundation chain.

Fold front corners of neck edge down as shown below and secure in place with a couple of hand stitches.

Tie drawstring ends together at centre front neck.

SUMMER CAP

The Summer Cap is simple and quick to make in easy treble crochet. Keep it plain for boys and brightly decorated for girls. Not only is it perfect for keeping unruly curls in place on a breezy day, but it will lend a certain je-ne-sais-quoi to any outfit.

BEFORE YOU BEGIN

SIZES AND MEASUREMENTS

To fit ages (in years)	2–3	3–4	4–5
Finished hat measurements			
Circumference	43cm	46cm	48cm
	17in	18in	19in
Length from centre top	16cm	17cm	18cm
	6½in	6¾in	7in

YARN

Pale Green Cap
Rowan *4-Ply Cotton* (50g/1¾ oz balls) as follows:

A pale green (Fresh 131)	1 ball	1 ball	1 ball
B turquoise (Aegean 129)	1 ball	1 ball	1 ball

Rowan *Cotton Glace* (50g/1¾ oz balls) as follows:

C red (Poppy 741)	1 ball	1 ball	1 ball

Mid Green Cap
Rowan *4-Ply Cotton* (50g/1¾ oz balls) as follows:

A mid green (Fennel 135)	1 ball	1 ball	1 ball
B pale green (Fresh 131)	1 ball	1 ball	1 ball

Rowan *Cotton Glace* (50g/1¾ oz balls) as follows:

C red (Poppy 741)	1 ball	1 ball	1 ball

Blue Cap
Rowan *4-Ply Cotton* (50g/1¾ oz balls) as follows:

A navy (Navy 150)	1 ball	1 ball	1 ball
B turquoise (Aegean 129)	1 ball	1 ball	1 ball

HOOKS
3.00mm (US size D-3) crochet hook
2.50mm (US size C-2) crochet hook

TENSION
23 tr and 13 rows to 10cm/4in measured over tr using A and 3.00mm (US size D-3) crochet hook *or size necessary to obtain correct tension.*

ABBREVIATIONS
See page 110.

GETTING STARTED

PALE GREEN CAP

TO MAKE CAP
Using 3.00mm (US size D-3) hook and A, make 6 ch and join with a ss to first ch to form a ring.
Round 1 (RS) 3 ch (to count as first tr), 15 tr in ring, join with a ss to 3rd of 3-ch, turn. *16 sts.*
(**Note:** First 3-ch of each round counts as first tr. Remember to turn at the end of each round.)
Round 2 3 ch, 1 tr in same place as ss, 2 tr in each tr to end, join with a ss to 3rd of 3-ch, turn. *32 sts.*
Round 3 3 ch, 1 tr in each tr to end, join with a ss to 3rd of 3-ch, turn.
Round 4 3 ch, 2 tr in next tr, [1 tr in next tr, 2 tr in next tr] 15 times, join with a ss to 3rd of 3-ch, turn. *48 sts.*
Round 5 3 ch, 1 tr in next tr, 2 tr in next tr, [1 tr in each of next 2 tr, 2 tr in next tr] 15 times, join with a ss to 3rd of 3-ch, turn. *64 sts.*
Round 6 3 ch, 1 tr in each tr to end, join with a ss to 3rd of 3-ch, turn.
Round 7 3 ch, 1 tr in each of next 2 tr, 2 tr in next tr, [1 tr in each of next 3 tr, 2 tr in next tr] 15 times, join with a ss to 3rd of 3-ch, turn. *80 sts.*
Round 8 3 ch, 1 tr in each of next 2 tr, 2 tr in next tr, [1 tr in each of next 3 tr, 2 tr in next tr] 19 times, join with a ss to 3rd of 3-ch, turn. *100 sts.*

1st size only:
Round 9 3 ch, 1 tr in each tr to end, join with a ss to 3rd of 3-ch, turn. *100 sts.*

2nd size only:
Round 9 3 ch, 1 tr in each of next 18 tr, 2 tr in next tr, [1 tr in each of next 19 tr, 2 tr in next tr] 4 times, join with a ss to 3rd of 3-ch, turn. *105 sts.*

3rd size only:
Round 9 3 ch, 1 tr in each of next 8 tr, 2 tr in next tr, [1 tr in each of next 9 tr, 2 tr in next tr] 9 times, join with a ss to 3rd of 3-ch, turn. *110 sts.*

All sizes:
Round 10 3 ch, 1 tr in each tr to end, join with a

ss to 3rd of 3-ch, turn.
Rep last round 11 (12: 13) times more. Fasten off.

DECORATIVE DOUBLE RINGS (make 7)

Using 2.50mm (US size C-2) hook and B, make
12 ch and join with a ss to first ch to form a ring.
Round 1 3 ch (to count as first tr), 11 tr in ring,
join with a ss to 3rd of 3-ch. Fasten off to
complete first section of double ring.
Using 2.50mm (US size C-2) crochet hook and C,
make 12 ch, pass hook through first section of
double ring and join with a ss to first ch to form
a ring linked around first ring.
Round 1 3 ch (to count as first tr), 11 tr in ring,
join with a ss to 3rd of 3-ch. Fasten off to
complete double ring.
Make 6 more double rings in
same way.

TO FINISH

Press pieces lightly
on wrong
side, following
instructions on
yarn label.

Cap edging

With RS facing
and using
2.50mm (US
size C-2) hook
and C, work
edging along
last row of cap
as follows:

Round 1 (RS) Join C with a ss to any tr, 1 ch,
1 dc in same place as ss, 1 dc in each st to end,
join with a ss to first dc.
Fasten off.

Decorative double rings

Sew rings to cap,
equally spaced
and about
2cm/¾in from
edge.

MID GREEN CAP

TO MAKE CAP
Make and finish as for Pale Green Cap.

BLUE CAP

TO MAKE CAP
Make and finish as for Pale Green Cap, but omitting decorative double rings and working cap edging in B.

WILBUR WHALE

Wilbur Whale loves the deep blue sea and is incredibly happy down there swimming about. There is nothing complicated about making Wilbur as he is made in three simple pieces in double crochet with easy embroidery and little button eyes.

BEFORE YOU BEGIN

SIZE
The finished toy whale measures approximately 22cm/8¾in long by 11.5cm/4½in tall.

YARN
Blue Whale
Rowan *4-Ply Cotton* (50g/1¾oz balls) as follows:

A navy (Navy 150)		1 ball
B turquoise (Aegean 129)		1 ball

Rowan *Cotton Glace* (50g/1¾oz balls) as follows:

C red (Poppy 741)		small amount

Turquoise Whale
Rowan *4-Ply Cotton* (50g/1¾oz balls) as follows:

A turquoise (Aegean 129)		1 ball
B navy (Navy 150)		1 ball

Rowan *Cotton Glace* (50g/1¾oz balls) as follows:

C red (Poppy 741)		small amount

HOOK
2.50mm (US size C-2) crochet hook

EXTRAS
Toy filling
2 buttons 11mm/⁷⁄₁₆in in diameter, for eyes

TENSION
23 sts and 30 rows to 10cm/4in measured over dc using A and 2.50mm (US size C-2) crochet hook *or size necessary to obtain correct tension.*

ABBREVIATIONS
dc2tog = [insert hook in next st, yrh and draw a loop through] twice, yrh and draw through all 3 loops on hook — *one st decreased.*
See also page 110.

GETTING STARTED

BODY – LEFT SIDE Ⓐ
Each side of the whale's body is worked from the front end to the tail.
Using 2.50mm (US size C-2) hook and A, make 27 ch.
Foundation row (RS) 1 dc in 2nd ch from hook, 1 dc in each of rem ch, turn. *26 dc.*
Row 1 1 ch (does NOT count as a st), 2 dc in first dc, 1 dc in each dc to last 2 dc, 2 dc in each of last 2 dc, turn. *29 dc.*
To help keep track of which is RS of piece, after turning work and before beg next row, mark this side of work as RS with a coloured thread.
Row 2 (RS) 1 ch, 2 dc in first dc, 1 dc in each dc to last dc, 2 dc in last dc, turn. *31 dc.*
Row 3 1 ch, 1 dc in each dc to end, turn.
Row 4 1 ch, 1 dc in each dc to last dc, 2 dc in last dc, turn. *32 dc.*
Row 5 1 ch, 1 dc in each dc to end, turn.
Rows 6–48 [Rep row 5] 43 times.
Row 49 1 ch, work dc2tog over first 2 dc, 1 dc in each dc to end, turn. *31 dc.*
Row 50 Rep row 5.
Row 51 Rep row 49. *30 dc.*
Row 52 1 ch, 1 dc in each dc to last 2 dc, work dc2tog over last 2 dc, turn. *29 dc.*
Row 53 1 ch, work dc2tog over first 2 dc, 1 dc in each dc to last 4 dc, [work dc2tog over next 2 dc] twice, turn. *26 dc.*
Row 54 1 ch, miss first dc, [work dc2tog over next 2 dc] twice, 1 dc in each dc to last 4 dc, [work dc2tog over next 2 dc] twice, turn. *21 dc.*
Row 55 1 ch, [work dc2tog over next 2 dc] twice, 1 dc in each dc to last 4 dc, [work dc2tog over next 2 dc] twice, turn. *17 dc.*
Fasten off.

Shape tail
With RS facing, work tail by rejoining A to sts as follows:
Row 56 (RS) Miss first 7 dc and rejoin A with a ss to next dc, 1 ch, 1 dc in same place as ss, 1 dc in each of next 3 dc, turn. *4 dc.*

Row 57 1 ch, 2 dc in first dc, 1 dc in each dc to last dc, 2 dc in last dc, turn. *6 dc.*
Rows 58–66 [Rep row 57] 9 times. *24 dc.*
Fasten off.

BODY – RIGHT SIDE

Using 2.50mm (US size C-2) hook and A, make 27 ch.
Foundation row (RS) 1 dc in 2nd ch from hook, 1 dc in each of rem ch, turn. *26 dc.*
Row 1 1 ch (does NOT count as a st), 2 dc in each of first 2 dc, 1 dc in each dc to last dc, 2 dc in last dc, turn. *29 dc.*
To help keep track of which is RS of piece, after turning work and before beg next row, mark this side of work as RS with a coloured thread.
Row 2 (RS) 1 ch, 2 dc in first dc, 1 dc in each dc to last dc, 2 dc in last dc, turn. *31 dc.*
Row 3 1 ch, 1 dc in each dc to end, turn.
Row 4 1 ch, 2 dc in first dc, 1 dc in each dc to

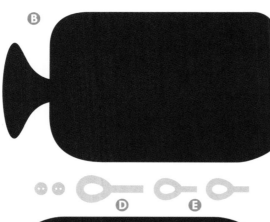

end, turn. *32 dc.*
Row 5 1 ch, 1 dc in each dc to end, turn.
Rows 6–48 [Rep row 5] 43 times.
Row 49 1 ch, 1 dc in each dc to last 2 dc, work dc2tog over last 2 dc, turn. *31 dc.*
Row 50 Rep row 5.
Row 51 Rep row 49. *30 dc.*
Row 52 1 ch, work dc2tog over first 2 dc, 1 dc in each dc to end, turn. *29 dc.*
Row 53 1 ch, [work dc2tog over next 2 dc] twice, 1 dc in each dc to last 2 dc, work dc2tog over last 2 dc, turn. *26 dc.*
Row 54 1 ch, [work dc2tog over next 2 dc] twice, 1 dc in each dc to last 5 dc, work dc2tog over next 2 dc, work dc2tog over next dc and last dc (missing dc in between), turn. *21 dc.*
Row 55 1 ch, [work dc2tog over next 2 dc] twice, 1 dc in each dc to last 4 dc, [work dc2tog over next 2 dc] twice, turn. *17 dc.*
Fasten off.

Shape tail
With RS facing, work tail by rejoining A to sts as follows:
Row 56 (RS) Miss first 6 dc and rejoin A with a ss to next dc, 1 ch, 1 dc in same place as ss, 1 dc in each of next 3 dc, turn. *4 dc.*
Row 57 1 ch, 2 dc in first dc, 1 dc in each dc to last dc, 2 dc in last dc, turn. *6 dc.*
Rows 58–66 [Rep row 57] 9 times. *24 dc.*
Fasten off.

UNDERBODY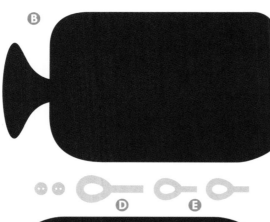

The underbody of the whale is worked from the mouth to the tail-end of the whale.
Using 2.50mm (US size C-2) hook and A, make 3 ch.
Foundation row (RS) 1 dc in 2nd ch from hook, 1 dc in last ch, turn. *2 dc.*
Row 1 1 ch (does NOT count as a st), 2 dc in first dc, 2 dc in last dc, turn. *4 dc.*
Row 2 1 ch, 2 dc in first dc, 1 dc in each dc to last dc, 2 dc in last dc, turn. *6 dc.*
Row 3 1 ch, 1 dc in each dc to end, turn.
Row 4 1 ch, 2 dc in first dc, 1 dc in each dc to last dc, 2 dc in last dc, turn. *8 dc.*
Row 5 1 ch, 1 dc in each dc to end, turn.
Rows 6–48 [Rep row 5] 43 times.

44

Row 49 1 ch, work dc2tog over first 2 dc, 1 dc in each dc to last 2 dc, work dc2tog over last 2 dc, turn. 6 dc.

Row 50 Rep row 5.

Row 51 Rep row 49. 4 dc.

Row 52 1 ch, work dc2tog over first 2 dc, work dc2tog over last 2 dc, turn. 2 dc.

Fasten off.

LONG WATER SPOUT Ⓓ

Using 2.50mm (US size C-2) hook and B, make 20 ch.

Row 1 1 ss in 2nd ch from hook, 1 dc in next ch, 1 htr in next ch, 1 tr in each of next 10 ch, 1 htr in next ch, 1 dc in next ch, join with a ss to side of first ss of row to form a loop, then work 1 ss in each of last 4 ch.

Fasten off.

SHORT WATER SPOUT Ⓔ (make 2)

Using 2.50mm (US size C-2) hook and B, make 16 ch.

Row 1 1 ss in 2nd ch from hook, 1 dc in next ch, 1 htr in next ch, 1 tr in each of next 6 ch, 1 htr in next ch, 1 dc in next ch, join with a ss to side of first ss of row to form a loop, then work 1 ss in each of last 4 ch.

Fasten off.

TO FINISH

Press pieces lightly on wrong side, following instructions on yarn label.

Bullion knot embroidery

Using a blunt-ended yarn needle, work five lines of bullion knots on both the right and left sides of the whale's body. Work each knot over one dc and work them one dc apart. Position the lines as follows:

Using B, work five bullion knots between 17th and 18th rows from foundation chain, working from right to left and working first knot over 13th dc from right side-edge.

Using B, work second line of bullion knots six rows above first line of knots. Begin second line of knots over 5th dc from right side-edge and work a total of 12 knots.

Work third and fourth lines of bullion knots in same way as second, each six rows above previous line of knots.

Work five bullion knots on fifth and final line of bullion knots as for first row and six rows above previous line of knots.

Cross-stitch embroidery

Using a blunt-ended yarn needle, work four lines of cross stitches (each over a long straight stitch) on both right and left sides of whale's body as follows:

Using B, work a long straight stitch between first two lines of bullion knots, working the stitch over 27 stitches and between 3rd and 4th rows (of the six rows between the lines of knots). Then using C, miss the first dc the straight stitch is worked over and work a cross stitch over the next dc and over two rows so that the straight stitch is at centre of cross stitch. Work 12 more cross stitches in the same way, each one dc apart. In the remaining spaces between rows of bullion knots, work three more lines of cross stitches in the same way as the first.

Whale seams

With wrong sides together, sew together tail sections of sides of body and fill tail firmly with toy filling.

Sew underbelly to sides of body, between foundation rows and 52nd rows. Sew remainder of seam to tail. Sew seam along top of whale, catching in ends of water spouts into seam as shown (see page 43).

Fill body firmly with toy filling, then sew foundation-row edges together at front of whale.

Eyes

For eyes, sew one small button to each side of body as shown.

Mouth

Using C for Blue Whale or B for Turquoise Whale, embroider mouth in backstitch as shown.

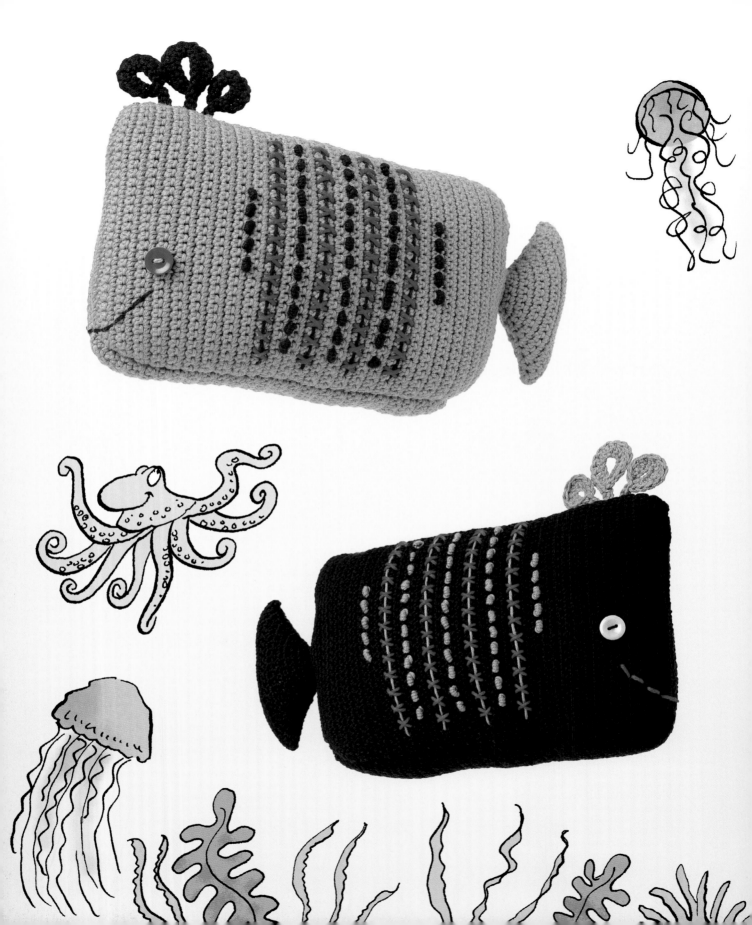

BEST BEACH BAG

This lovely little bag is made in no time at all. It is essential for carrying all those bits and bobs and odds and ends that you will need or find when you take a trip to the beach. If you are worried that all your treasures might slip through the holes, you could stitch a simple lining into it.

BEFORE YOU BEGIN

SIZE
The finished bag measures approximately 15cm/6in wide by 16cm/6½in deep.

YARN
Rowan *4-Ply Cotton* (50g/1¾ oz balls) as follows:

A	pale green (Fresh 131)	1 ball
B	turquoise (Aegean 129)	1 ball
C	navy (Navy 150)	1 ball

Rowan *Cotton Glace* (50g/1¾ oz balls) as follows:

D	red (Poppy 741)	1 ball

HOOK
2.50mm (US size C-2) crochet hook

TENSION
One motif measures 5cm/2in square using 2.50mm (US size C-2) crochet hook or *size necessary to obtain correct tension*.

ABBREVIATIONS
See page 110.

GETTING STARTED

MOTIFS (make 18)
Using 2.50mm (US size C-2) hook and A, make 6 ch and join with a ss to first ch to form a ring.
Round 1 (RS) 3 ch (to count as first tr), 15 tr in ring, join with a ss to 3rd of 3-ch. *16 sts.*
Fasten off.
(Do not turn at end of rounds, but work with RS always facing.)
Round 2 Join D with a ss to any tr, 1 ch, 1 dc in same place as ss, *3 ch, miss next tr, 1 dc in next tr; rep from * 6 times more, 3 ch, join with a ss to first dc.
Fasten off.
Round 3 Join B with a ss to any 3-ch sp, 3 ch (to count as first tr), [2 tr, 2 ch, 3 tr] all in same 3-ch sp as ss, *2 tr in next 3-ch sp, [3 tr, 2 ch, 3 tr] all in next 3-ch sp; rep from * twice more, 2 tr in next 3-ch sp, join with a ss to 3rd of 3-ch.
Fasten off.
Round 4 Join C with a ss to any tr, 1 ch, 1 dc in same place as ss, then work 1 dc in each tr and 2 dc in each 2-ch sp (corner) to end of round, join with a ss to first dc. Fasten off.

EDGING PIECES (make 2)
Using 2.50mm (US size C-2) hook and C, make 33 ch.
Foundation row 1 dc in 2nd ch from hook, 1 dc in each of rem ch, turn. *32 dc.*
Row 1 1 ch (does NOT count as a st), 1 dc in each dc to end, turn.
Row 2 Rep row 1.
Fasten off.

HANDLES (make 2)
Using 2.50mm (US size C-2) hook and C, make 43 ch.
Foundation round (WS) 1 dc in 2nd ch from hook, 1 dc in each ch to last ch, 2 dc in last ch, then working along other side of foundation ch, miss first ch, 1 dc in each of next 41 ch, join with a ss to first dc, turn. *84 dc.*
Round 1 1 ch (does NOT count as a st), 2 dc in first dc, 1 dc in each of next 40 dc, 2 dc in each of next 2 dc, 1 dc in each of next 40 dc, 2 dc in last dc, join with a ss to first dc. *88 dc.*
Fasten off.

TO FINISH
Press pieces lightly on wrong side, following instructions on yarn label.
To make front of bag, join nine motifs together to form a square three motifs wide by three motifs deep. To do this, hold motifs together and

work a dc through each pair of adjacent stitches, leaving the 2 dc at each corner of each motif free.

Make back of bag in same way with remaining nine motifs.

Holding top of front of bag and last row of one edging piece together, join them as follows:

Miss first dc on edging and 2 corner dc on first motif square, then *[work 1 dc in next dc on both layers] 8 times, miss next 3 dc on edging and 2 corner dc of next motif; rep from * once more, [work 1 dc in next dc on both layers] 8 times. Fasten off.

Join back of bag to remaining edging piece in same way.

Join front to back in same way.

Fold each handle in half lengthways and sew together along side edge.

Sew one handle to top of edging on front of bag, with each end 2.5cm/1in from side seam. Sew remaining handle to back of bag in same way.

DOLORES DRESS

Dolores likes wearing this dress for special occasions as it is so simple and classic. Dainty edgings, pretty buttons, sweet pockets and a lovely belt make it very special indeed. Wear it with the Dolores Slippers (see page 58) for the perfect party outfit.

SIZES AND MEASUREMENTS

To fit ages (in years)	2–3	3–4	4–5
To fit chest	56cm	61cm	66cm
	22in	24in	26in
Finished measurements			
Around chest	66cm	73cm	79cm
	26in	28¾in	31in
Length to shoulder	50cm	56cm	64cm
	19¾in	22in	25¼in

YARN

Rowan *4-Ply Soft* (50g/1¾oz balls) as follows:

A	sage green (Leafy 367)	7 balls	7 balls	8 balls
B	red (Honk 374)	1 ball	1 ball	1 ball
C	pink (Fairy 395)	1 ball	1 ball	1 ball
D	pale blue (Whisper 370)	1 ball	1 ball	1 ball

HOOK

2.50mm (US size C-2) crochet hook

EXTRAS

4 yellow buttons 15mm/⅝in in diameter

TENSION

25 sts and 18 rows to 10cm/4in measured over main patt using 2.50mm (US size C-2) crochet hook *or size necessary to obtain correct tension.*
25 sts and 26 rows to 10cm/4in measured over dc using 2.50mm (US size C-2) crochet hook *or size necessary to obtain correct tension.*

ABBREVIATIONS

dc2tog = [insert hook in next st, yrh and draw a loop through] twice, yrh and draw through all 3 loops on hook — *one st decreased.*

tr2tog = [yrh and insert hook in next st, yrh and draw a loop through, yrh and draw a loop through 2 loops on hook] twice, yrh and draw through all 3 loops on hook — *one st decreased.* See also page 110.

BACK

Using 2.50mm (US size C-2) hook and A, make 111 (123: 135) ch.

Foundation row (RS) 1 htr in 5th ch from hook, *1 ch, miss 1 ch, 1 htr in next ch; rep from * to end, turn. *109 (121: 133) sts.*

Row 1 1 ch (does NOT count as a st), 1 dc in first htr, *1 dc in next ch sp, 1 dc in next htr; rep from * to end, 1 dc in next ch sp, 1 dc in 3rd of 4-ch, turn. *109 (121: 133) dc.*

Row 2 3 ch (to count as first htr and first ch sp), miss first 2 dc, 1 htr in next dc, *1 ch, miss 1 dc, 1 htr in next dc; rep from * to end.

Row 3 1 ch, 1 dc in first htr, *1 dc in next ch sp, 1 dc in next htr; rep from * to end, 1 dc in next ch sp, 1 dc in 2nd of 3-ch, turn.

Beg main patt as follows:

Main patt row 1 (RS) 3 ch (to count as first tr), miss first dc, 1 tr in each dc to end, turn.

Main patt row 2 1 ch (does NOT count as a st), 1 dc in each tr to end, 1 dc in 3rd of 3-ch, turn. (Last 2 rows form main patt when repeated.)

Next row (dec row) (RS) 3 ch, miss first dc, 1 tr in each of next 6 dc, work tr2tog over next 2 dc, 1 tr in each dc to last 9 dc, work tr2tog over next 2 dc, 1 tr in each of next 7 dc, turn.
Work straight in main patt for 3 rows.
Rep last 4 rows 10 (12:14) times more and then the dec row again, ending with a RS row. *85 (93: 101) sts.*

Next row (WS) 1 ch, 1 dc in each tr to end, 1 dc in 3rd of 3-ch, turn.

Shape bodice

Next row (RS) 1 ch (does NOT count as a st), 1 dc in each dc to end, turn.
(Last row forms simple dc patt when repeated.)

Working bodice in dc throughout, work straight for 5 rows.

Next row (dec row) 1 ch, 1 dc in first dc, 1 dc in each of next 6 dc, work dc2tog over next 2 dc, 1 dc in each dc to last 9 dc, work dc2tog over next 2 dc, 1 dc in each of last 7 dc, turn. 83 (91: 99) dc.

Work straight until Back measures 38 (43: 50) cm/ 15 (17: 19¾) in from beg, ending with a RS row.

Shape armholes

Next row (WS) 1 ss in each of first 6 (7: 8) dc, 1 ch, 1 dc in same place as last ss, 1 dc in each dc to last 5 (6: 7) dc, turn. 73 (79: 85) dc.

Next row 1 ch, 1 dc in first dc, work dc2tog over next 2 dc, 1 dc in each dc to last 3 dc, work dc2tog over next 2 dc, 1 dc in last dc, turn.

Rep last row 4 times more. 63 (69: 75) dc.**

Work straight until Back measures 48 (54: 62) cm/ 19 (21¼: 24½) in from beg, ending with a WS row.

Shape back neck

Next row (RS) 1 ch, 1 dc in first dc, 1 dc in each of next 15 (17: 19) dc, turn.

Work straight for 4 rows.

Fasten off.

With RS facing, return to sts left unworked, miss centre 31 (33: 35) dc and rejoin A with a ss to next dc, 1 ch, 1 dc in same place as ss, 1 dc in each dc to end, turn.

Work straight for 4 rows.

Fasten off.

FRONT

Work as for Back to **.

Work straight until Front measures 44 (50: 58) cm/ 17¼ (19¾ : 22¾) in from beg, ending with a WS row.

Shape front neck

Next row (RS) 1 ch, 1 dc in first dc, 1 dc in each of next 15 (17: 19) dc, turn.

Work straight until Front measures same as Back to shoulder.

Fasten off.

With RS facing, return to sts left unworked, miss centre 31 (33: 35) dc and rejoin A with a ss to next dc, 1 ch, 1 dc in same place as ss, 1 dc in each dc to end, turn.

Work straight until Front measures same as Back to shoulder.

Fasten off.

SLEEVES (make 2)

Using 2.50mm (US size C-2) hook and A, make 67 (73: 79) ch.

Foundation row (RS) 1 htr in 5th ch from hook, *1 ch, miss 1 ch, 1 htr in next ch; rep from * to end, turn. 65 (71: 77) sts.

Row 1 1 ch (does NOT count as a st), 1 dc in first htr, *1 dc in next ch sp, 1 dc in next htr; rep from * to end, 1 dc in next ch sp, 1 dc in 3rd of 4-ch, turn. 65 (71: 77) dc.

Row 2 3 ch (to count as first htr and first ch sp), miss first 2 dc, 1 htr in next dc, *1 ch, miss 1 dc, 1 htr in next dc; rep from * to end.

Row 3 1 ch, 1 dc in first htr, *1 dc in next ch sp, 1 dc in next htr; rep from * to end, 1 dc in next ch sp, 1 dc in 2nd of 3-ch, turn.

Row 4 1 ch, 1 dc in each dc to end, turn.

(Last row forms simple dc patt when repeated.)

Cont in dc throughout, beg sleeve shaping as follows:

Next row (inc row) 1 ch, 1 dc in each of first 3 dc, 2 dc in next dc, 1 dc in each dc to last 4 dc, 2 dc in next dc, 1 dc in each of last 3 dc, turn.

Work straight for 2 rows.

Rep last 3 rows 0 (1: 2) times more.

Next row (inc row) 1 ch, 1 dc in each of first 3 dc, 2 dc in next dc, 1 dc in each dc to last 4 dc, 2 dc in next dc, 1 dc in each of last 3 dc, turn. 69 (77: 85) dc.

Work straight for 3 (2: 1) rows.

Shape top of sleeve

Next row 1 ss in each of first 6 (7: 8) dc, 1 ch, 1 dc in same place as last ss, 1 dc in each dc to last 5 (6: 7) dc, turn. 59 (65: 71) dc.

Next row 1 ch, 1 dc in first dc, work dc2tog over next 2 dc, 1 dc in each dc to last 3 dc, work dc2tog over next 2 dc, 1 dc in last dc, turn.

Rep last row 4 times more. 49 (55: 61) dc.

Fasten off.

POCKETS (make 2)

Using 2.50mm (US size C-2) hook and A, make 20 ch.

Foundation row (RS) 1 dc in 2nd ch from hook, 1 dc in each of rem ch, turn. *19 dc.*

Row 1 (patt row) 1 ch, 1 dc in each dc to end, turn.

(Last row forms simple dc patt when repeated.)

Row 2 (inc row) 1 ch, 1 dc in each of first 3 dc, *2 dc in next dc, 1 dc in each of next 2 dc; rep from * 3 times more, 2 dc in next dc, 1 dc in each of last 3 dc, turn. *24 dc.*

Cont in dc throughout, work straight for 5 rows, ending with a WS row.

Next row (inc row) (RS) 1 ch, 1 dc in each of first 2 dc, *2 dc in next dc, 1 dc in each of next 2 dc; rep from * 5 times more, 2 dc in next dc, 1 dc in each of last 3 dc, turn. *31 dc.*

Work straight for 5 rows, ending with a WS row.

Next row (dec row) (RS) 1 ch, 1 dc in each of first 2 dc, *work dc2tog over next 2 dc, 1 dc in each of next 2 dc; rep from * 5 times more, work dc2tog over next 2 dc, 1 dc in each of last 3 dc. *24 dc.*

Fasten off.

Edging

With RS facing for each of the 4 rows of the pocket edging, join on a new colour on each row as follows:

Next row (RS) Join D with a ss to first dc, 1 ch, 1 dc in same dc as ss, 1 dc in each dc to end.

Fasten off.

Rep last row 3 times more, working one row each in A, C and B.

BELT

Using 2.50mm (US size C-2) hook and B, make 220 (240: 260) ch.

Foundation row (RS) 1 dc in 2nd ch from hook, 1 dc in each of rem ch.

Fasten off.

With RS facing for each of rem 6 rows of belt, join on a new colour on each row as follows:

Row 1 (RS) Join C with a ss to first dc, 1 ch (does NOT count as a st), 1 dc in same dc as ss, 1 dc in each dc to end.

Fasten off.

Row 2 (RS) Using A, rep row 1.

Fasten off.

Row 3 (buttonhole row) (RS) Join D with a ss to first dc, 1 ch, 1 dc in same dc as ss, 3 ch, miss next 3 dc, 1 dc in each of next 18 dc, 3 ch, miss next 3 dc, 1 dc in each dc to end.

Fasten off.

Row 4 (RS) Join A with a ss to first dc, 1 ch, 1 dc in same dc as ss, then work 1 dc in each dc and 3 dc in each 3-ch sp to end.

Fasten off.

Row 5 (RS) Using C, rep row 1.

Fasten off.

Work final row of belt along row-end edges (short side edges) of belt and along top of previous row as follows:

Row 6 (RS) Join B with a ss to end of foundation row at right end of belt, 1 ch, 1 dc in same place as ss, 1 dc in each row-end to corner, 2 dc in first dc of previous row, 1 dc in each dc to last dc, 2 dc in last dc, 1 dc in each row-end along this end of belt.

Fasten off.

BELT CARRIERS (make 3)

Using 2.50mm (US size C-2) hook and A, make 7 ch.

Foundation row (RS) 1 dc in 2nd ch from hook, 1 dc in each of rem ch, turn. *6 dc.*

Row 1 1 ch (does NOT count as a st), 1 dc in each dc to end.

Fasten off.

TO FINISH

Press pieces lightly on wrong side, following instructions on yarn label.

Sew shoulder seams.

Sew sleeves to armholes. Sew side and sleeve seams.

Lower edging

With RS facing and using 2.50mm (US size C-2) hook and C, work edging along foundation-chain edges of Front and Back as follows:

Round 1 (RS) Join C with a ss to foundation-chain edge of Front at right side seam, 1 ch, 1 dc in same place as ss, 1 dc in each foundation ch to end, join with a ss to first dc.

Fasten off.

(Do not turn at end of round, but cont with RS facing.)

Round 2 Join B with a ss to first dc, *5 ch, 1 ss in first ch, 1 dc in each of next 3 dc; rep from * to end, join with a ss to first ch. Fasten off.

Sleeve edging
With RS facing and using 2.50mm (US size C-2) hook, join C to foundation-chain edge of Sleeve at sleeve seam and work edging as for lower edging.

Sew pockets to front of dress as shown right, stitching them in place with side edges parallel so that top of pocket puffs outwards.

Sew one belt carrier to each side seam and one to centre back. Thread belt through carriers. Sew two buttons to belt to fit.

Sew two buttons below neck for decoration as shown right.

DOLORES SLIPPERS

You will never want to take these dainty little Dolores Slippers off as they are beautifully comfortable and very practical. They really will keep your feet warm on chilly autumn days. Dress them up with the sweetest button you can find – lovely!

SIZES AND MEASUREMENTS

To fit ages (in years)	2–3	3–4	4–5
Length of slippers	14.5cm	16cm	17.5cm
	5¾ in	6¼ in	6¾ in

YARN

Rowan *4-Ply Soft* (50g/1¾ oz balls) as follows:

A	sea green (Folly 391)	1 ball	1 ball	1 ball
B	charcoal (Sooty 372)	1 ball	1 ball	1 ball

Small amount of each of the following colours:
C red (Honk 374)
D pink (Fairy 395)
E sage green (Leafy 391)
F pale blue (Whisper 370)

HOOK

2.50mm (US size C-2) crochet hook

EXTRAS

2 small buttons

TENSION

25 sts and 26 rows to 10cm/4in measured over dc using 2.50mm (US size C-2) crochet hook or *size necessary to obtain correct tension.*

ABBREVIATIONS

See page 110.

SLIPPERS (make 2)

Using 2.50mm (US size C-2) hook and A, make 21 ch.

Sole

Foundation round (WS) 1 dc in 2nd ch from hook, 1 dc in each ch to last ch, 3 dc in last ch, then working along other side of foundation ch, miss first ch, 1 dc in each of last 19 ch, join with a ss to first ch, turn. *41 dc.*

(**Note:** When working the rounds, the work is turned at the heel-end of the sole. Remember to turn at end of each round.)

Round 1 (RS) 1 ch (does NOT count as a st), 2 dc in first dc, 1 dc in each of next 18 dc, 2 dc in each of next 3 dc, 1 dc in each of next 18 dc, 2 dc in last dc, join with a ss to 1-ch, turn. *46 dc.*

Round 2 1 ch, 2 dc in first dc, 1 dc in each of next 20 dc, 2 dc in each of next 4 dc, 1 dc in each of next 20 dc, 2 dc in last dc, join with a ss to 1-ch, turn. *52 dc.*

Do not cut off yarn, but leave a long loop to return to.

With RS facing, join in a spare length of A on next row and work 2 extra rows of shaping at toe-end of sole as follows:

Next row (RS) Using a spare length of A, miss first 17 dc and join on yarn with a ss to next dc, 1 ch, 1 ss in same place as first ss, 1 dc in each of next 7 dc, 2 dc in each of next 2 dc, 1 dc in each of next 7 dc, 1 ss in next dc, turn.

Next row 1 ss in next dc, 1 dc in each of next 7 dc, 2 dc in each of next 2 dc, 1 dc in each of next 7 dc, 1 ss in next dc, turn. *56 sts all around sole.*

Cut off spare length of A.

Return to main ball of A and work next round as follows:

Round 3 (RS) 1 ch, 2 dc in first dc, 1 dc in each of next 26 sts, 2 dc in each of next 2 dc, 1 dc in each of next 26 sts, 2 dc in last dc, join with a ss to 1-ch, turn. *60 dc.*

Do not cut off yarn, but leave a long loop to return to.

Again work 2 extra rows of shaping at toe-end of sole as follows:

Next row (WS) Using a spare length of A, miss first 13 dc and join on yarn with a ss to next dc, 1 ch, 1 ss in same place as first ss, 1 dc in each of next 15 dc, 2 dc in each of next 2 dc, 1 dc in each of next 15 dc, 1 ss in next dc, turn.

Next row 1 ss in next dc, 1 dc in each of next 15 dc, 2 dc in each of next 2 dc, 1 dc in each of next 15 dc, 1 ss in next dc, turn. *64 sts all around sole.*

Cut off spare length of A.

Return to main ball of A and work next round as follows:

Round 4 (WS) 1 ch, 2 dc in first dc, 1 dc in each of next 30 sts, 2 dc in each of next 2 dc, 1 dc in each of next 30 sts, 2 dc in last dc, join with a ss to 1-ch, turn. *68 dc.*

Do not cut off yarn, but leave a long loop to return to.

Again work 2 extra rows of shaping at toe-end of sole as follows:

Next row (RS) Using a spare length of A, miss first 9 dc and join on yarn with a ss to next dc, 1 ch, 1 ss in same place as first ss, 1 dc in each of next 23 dc, 2 dc in each of next 2 dc, 1 dc in each of next 23 dc, 1 ss in next dc, turn.

Next row 1 ss in next dc, 1 dc in each of next 23 dc, 2 dc in each of next 2 dc, 1 dc in each of next 23 dc, 1 ss in next dc, turn. *72 sts all around sole.*

Cut off spare length of A.

Return to main ball of A complete sole in rounds as follows:

Round 5 (RS) 1 ch, 2 dc in first dc, 1 dc in each of next 32 sts, 2 dc in next dc, 1 dc in each of next 4 dc, 2 dc in next dc, 1 dc in each of next 32 sts, 2 dc in last dc, join with a ss to 1-ch, turn. *76 dc.*

Round 6 1 ch, 2 dc in first dc, 1 dc in each of next 33 dc, 2 dc in next dc, 1 dc in each of next 6 dc, 2 dc in next dc, 1 dc in each of next 33 dc, 2 dc in last dc, join with a ss to 1-ch, turn. *80 dc.*
Work 2 (4: 6) rounds more in this way (as set by rounds 5 and 6), working each round with 1 dc more between increases along each side edge of sole and 2 dc more between increases at toe-end of sole, ending with a WS row. *88 (96: 104) dc.*

Cut off A.

Upper section of slipper
Change to B and cont as follows:

Next round Using B, 1 ch, 1 dc in each dc, join with a ss to 1-ch, turn.

Rep last round 4 (6: 8) times more, ending with a RS row.

Do not cut off yarn, but leave a long loop to return to.

With WS facing, join in a spare length of B on next row and work 6 extra rows of shaping at toe-end of slipper as follows:

Next row (WS) Using a spare length of B, miss first 20 (22: 24) dc and join on yarn with a ss to next dc, 1 ch, 1 ss in same place as first ss, 1 dc in each of next 22 (24: 26) dc, miss next 2 dc, 1 dc in each of next 22 (24: 26) dc, 1 ss in next dc, turn.

Next row 1 ss in next dc, 1 dc in each of next 20 (22: 24) dc, miss next 2 dc, 1 dc in each of next 20 (22: 24) dc, 1 ss in next dc, turn.

Next row 1 ss in next dc, 1 dc in each of next 18 (20: 22) dc, miss next 2 dc, 1 dc in each of next 18 (20: 22) dc, 1 ss in next dc, turn.

Next row 1 ss in next dc, 1 dc in each of next 16 (18: 20) dc, miss next 2 dc, 1 dc in each of next 16 (18: 20) dc, 1 ss in next dc, turn.

Next row 1 ss in next dc, 1 dc in each of next 14 (16: 18) dc, miss next 2 dc, 1 dc in each of next 14 (16: 18) dc, 1 ss in next dc, turn.

Next row 1 ss in next dc, 1 dc in each of next 12 (14: 16) dc, miss next 2 dc, 1 dc in each of next 12 (14: 16) dc, 1 ss in next dc, turn. *76 (84: 92) sts.*

Cut off spare length of B.

Return to main ball of B and work next round as follows:

Next round (WS) 1 ch, 1 dc in each of next 20 (22: 24) dc, 1 dc in each of next 6 ss, 1 dc in each of next 11 (13: 15) dc, miss next 2 dc, 1 dc in each of next 11 (13: 15) dc, 1 dc in each of next 6 ss, 1 dc in each of next 20 (22: 24) dc, join with a ss to 1-ch, turn.

Cut off B.

With RS always facing, cont in stripes as follows:

Next round (RS) Using C, 1 ch, 1 dc in each of first 36 (40: 44) dc, miss next 2 dc, 1 dc in each of next 36 (40: 44) dc, join with a ss to 1-ch, do not turn.

Cut off C.

Next round (RS) Using D, 1 ch, 1 dc in each of first 35 (39: 43) dc, miss next 2 dc, 1 dc in each of

next 35 (39: 43) dc, join with a ss to 1-ch, do not turn.
Cut off D.
Next round Using E, 1 ch, 1 dc in each of first 34 (38: 42) dc, miss next 2 dc, 1 dc in each of next 34 (38: 42) dc, join with a ss to 1-ch, do not turn.
Cut off E.
Next round Using F, 1 ch, 1 dc in each of first 33 (37: 41) dc, miss next 2 dc, 1 dc in each of next 33 (37: 41) dc, join with a ss to 1-ch, do not turn.
Fasten off.
With RS still facing, change to D and work two rows as follows:
Next row (RS) Miss first 26 (28: 30) dc, join D with a ss to next dc, 1 ch, 1 ss in same place as first ss, 1 dc in each of next 5 (7: 9) dc, miss next 2 dc, 1 dc in each of next 5 (7: 9) dc, 1 ss in next dc, turn.
Next row (WS) Using D, 1 ss in next dc, 1 dc in each of next 3 (5: 7) dc, miss next 2 dc, 1 dc in each of next 3 (5: 7) dc, 1 ss in next dc.

Fasten off.
With RS facing, return to beg of round and join C with a ss to first dc, 1 ch, 1 dc in same place as ss, then work in dc to end of round decreasing at toe as before, join with a ss to 1-ch.
Fasten off.

STRAPS (make 2)
Using 2.50mm (US size C-2) hook and C, make 41 (45: 49) ch.
Foundation round (RS) 1 dc in 7th ch from hook, 1 dc in each ch to last ch, 3 dc in last ch, then working along other side of foundation ch, miss first ch, 1 dc in each ch to last 6 ch (that form buttonhole loop), join with a ss to first dc.
Fasten off.

TO FINISH
Sew centre 16 dc of one strap to centre of back of each slipper.
Sew a button to end of strap on each slipper to correspond with buttonhole loop.

ARIADNE DOLL

Ariadne enjoys walking in the park with her little dog Hercule. They often go shopping together. Ariadne likes to buy flowers for herself and treats for Hercule.

SIZE
The finished doll measures approximately 34cm/13½in tall, including hat.

YARN
Rowan *4-Ply Soft* (50g/1¾oz balls) as follows:

Doll with red skirt
A	red (Honk 374)	1 ball
B	sea green (Folly 391)	1 ball
C	sage green (Leafy 367)	1 ball
D	charcoal (Sooty 372)	1 ball
E	ecru (Linseed 393)	1 ball
F	pink (Fairy 395)	small amount

Doll with pink skirt
A	pink (Fairy 395)	1 ball
B	red (Honk 374)	1 ball
C	sea green (Folly 391)	1 ball
D	charcoal (Sooty 372)	1 ball
E	ecru (Linseed 393)	1 ball

HOOKS
2.50mm (US size C-2) crochet hook
2.00mm (US size B-1) crochet hook

EXTRAS
1 button 11mm/⁷⁄₁₆in in diameter, to decorate belt

TENSION
25 sts and 26 rows to 10cm/4in measured over dc using 2.50mm (US size C-2) crochet hook *or size necessary to obtain correct tension.*

ABBREVIATIONS
dc2tog = [insert hook in next st, yrh and draw a loop through] twice, yrh and draw through all 3 loops on hook — *one st decreased.*
See also page 110.

DOLL WITH RED SKIRT

FRONT OF DOLL Ⓐ
The front and the back of the doll are each worked in one piece from the hem of the skirt to the top of the head. (The arms and legs are worked separately and stitched on later.)

Skirt
Using 2.50mm (US size C-2) hook and A, make 29 ch.
Foundation row (RS) 1 dc in 2nd ch from hook, 1 dc in each of rem ch, turn. *28 dc.*
Row 1 1 ch (does NOT count as a st), 1 dc in each dc to end, turn.
Rows 2 and 3 [Rep row 1] twice.
To help keep track of which is RS of piece, after turning work and before beg next row, mark this side of work as RS with a coloured thread.
Row 4 (dec row) (RS) 1 ch, work dc2tog over first 2 dc, 1 dc in each dc to last 2 dc, work dc2tog over last 2 dc, turn.
Rows 5–8 [Rep row 1] 4 times.
Rows 9–23 [Rep rows 4–8] 3 times. *20 dc.*
Row 24 Rep row 4. *18 dc.*
Rows 25–27 [Rep row 1] 3 times.
Cut off A.
This completes the skirt front.

Belt
Change to D and work doll's belt as follows:
Rows 28 and 29 [Rep row 1] twice.
Cut off D.

Jumper
Change to B and work front of doll's jumper as follows:
Rows 30–36 [Rep row 1] 7 times.
Row 37 Rep row 4. *16 dc.*
Rows 38–43 [Rep row 1] 6 times.
Row 44 Rep row 4.
Row 45 Rep row 1.
Rows 46–53 [Rep rows 44 and 45] 4 times. *6 dc.*
Cut off B.

Head

Change to E and work head as follows:

Row 54 Rep row 4. *4 dc.*

Row 55 Rep row 1.

Row 56 1 ch, 2 dc in first dc, 1 dc in each dc to last dc, 2 dc in last dc. *6 dc.*

Rows 57–59 [Rep row 56] 3 times. *12 dc.***

Rows 60 and 61 [Rep row 1] twice.

Nose and top of head

Row 62 (RS) 1 ch, 1 dc in each of first 6 dc, 5 ch (for nose), 1 ss in base of last dc, 1 dc in each of next 6 dc, turn.

Keeping nose on RS of work, complete head as follows:

Rows 63 and 64 [Rep row 1] twice.

Row 65 Rep row 4. *10 dc.*

Row 66 Rep row 1.

Rows 67–70 [Rep row 4] 4 times. *2 dc.*

Fasten off.

BACK OF DOLL B

Work as for front of doll to **.

Top of head

Rows 60–64 [Rep row 1] 5 times.

Row 65 Rep row 4. *10 dc.*

Row 66 Rep row 1.

Rows 67–70 [Rep row 4] 4 times. *2 dc.*

Fasten off.

LEGS C (make 2)

Each leg is worked in one piece from the shoe to the top of the leg.

Shoe section

Using 2.50mm (US size C-2) hook and C, make 7 ch and join with a ss to first ch to form a ring.

Round 1 (RS) 1 ch, 6 dc in ring.

(**Note:** The legs are worked in a spiral with RS always facing; so to keep track of where each round begins and ends, place a marker at end of each round.)

Round 2 1 dc in each dc to end of round.

Rounds 3–6 [Rep round 2] 4 times.

Cut off C.

Leg section

Change to E and rep round 2 until leg measures 10cm/4in from beg (including shoe section).

Fasten off.

ARMS D (make 2)

Each arm is worked in one piece from the hand to the top of the sleeve.

Hand section

Using 2.50mm (US size C-2) hook and E, make 7 ch and join with a ss to first ch to form a ring.

Round 1 (RS) 1 ch, 6 dc in ring.

(**Note:** The arms are worked in a spiral with RS

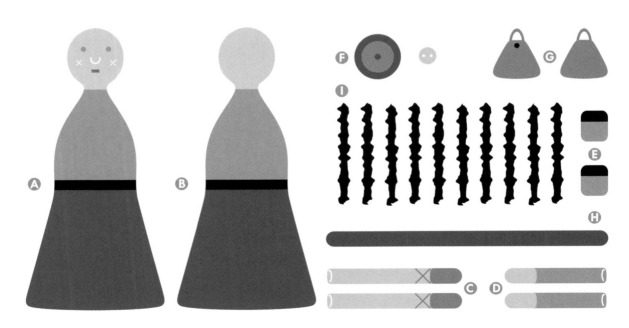

always facing until shaping for top of sleeve is reached; so to keep track of where each round begins and ends, place a marker at end of each round.)

Round 2 1 dc in each dc to end of round.
Rounds 3–7 [Rep round 2] 5 times.
Cut off E.

Sleeve
Change to B and work sleeve as follows:
Rounds 8–15 [Rep round 2] 8 times.
Round 16 1 dc in each dc to end of round, *turn*.

Shape top of sleeve
Work top of sleeve back and forth in rows as follows:
Next row (WS) 1 ch (does NOT count as a st), 1 dc in each of first 3 dc, turn.
Next row 1 ch, 1 dc in each of 3 dc, turn.
Rep last row once more.
Fasten off, leaving a long tail-end of yarn for sewing arm to body.

POCKETS **E** (make 2)
Using 2.50mm (US size C-2) hook and B, make 5 ch.
Foundation row (RS) 1 dc in 2nd ch from hook, 1 dc in each of rem ch, turn. *4 dc*.
Row 1 1 ch (does NOT count as a st), 1 dc in each dc to end, turn.
Rows 2 and 3 [Rep row 1] twice.
Cut off B.

Pocket top edging
Change to D and work edging as follows:
Rows 4 and 5 [Rep row 1] twice.
Fasten off.

HAT **F**
Using 2.50mm (US size C-2) hook and C, make 6 ch and join with a ss to first ch to form a ring.
Round 1 (RS) 1 ch, 5 dc in ring.
(**Note:** The hat is worked in a spiral with RS always facing; so to keep track of where each round begins and ends, place a marker at end of each round.)
Round 2 2 dc in each dc to end of round. *10 dc*.
Round 3 Rep round 2. *20 dc*.
Round 4 1 dc in each dc to end of round.

Round 5 Rep round 4.
Cut off C.

Hat edging
Change to A and work hat edging as follows:
Round 6 *1 dc in next dc, 2 dc in next dc; rep from * 9 times more.
Fasten off.

BAG PIECES **G** (make 2)
Using 2.50mm (US size C-2) hook and C, make 8 ch.
Foundation row (RS) 1 dc in 2nd ch from hook, 1 dc in each of rem ch, turn. *7 dc*.
Row 1 1 ch (does NOT count as a st), 1 dc in each dc to end, turn.
Row 2 Rep row 1.
Row 3 1 ch, work dc2tog over first 2 dc, 1 dc in each dc to last 2 dc, work dc2tog over last 2 dc, turn. *5 dc*.
Rows 4 and 5 [Rep row 1] twice.
Row 6 Rep row 3. *3 dc*.
Row 7 Rep row 1.

Handle
Row 8 10 ch, miss first 2 dc, 1 ss in last dc.
Fasten off.

SCARF **H**
Using 2.50mm (US size C-2) hook and A, make 60 ch.
Round 1 (RS) 1 dc in 2nd ch from hook, 1 dc in each ch to last ch, 2 dc in last ch, then working along other side of foundation ch, miss first ch, 1 dc in each ch to last ch, 1 ss in last ch.
Fasten off.

HAIR STRANDS **I** (make 10)
Using 2.00mm (US size B-1) hook and D, make 50 ch and fasten off.

TO FINISH
Do not press.

Face
Using a blunt-ended yarn needle for all embroidery, work face embroidery as follows:
For mouth, use A to work three straight stitches 2 dc wide on top of each other, positioning them two rows below nose.

For each eye, use B to work one bullion knot one row above nose and 2 dc from centre dc. For each cheek, use F to work a small cross stitch two rows below eye.

Pockets and belt

Sew pockets to front of skirt three rows below belt and 5 dc apart.
Sew button to centre of belt on front of doll.

Body

Leaving last three rows at top of jumper open and hem-edge of skirt open, sew back of body to front of body. Sew top of each sleeve to opening in seam at top of jumper.
Fill body firmly with toy filling.
Pin legs to centre of skirt hem and 3 dc apart so that about 3cm/1¼in of top of each leg will be inside of skirt; then sew together skirt-hem edges, catching in legs.

Shoe ribbons

Using C, embroider a large cross stitch above each shoe on front of doll, then a straight stitch across back of leg at top of cross stitch to imitate shoe ribbons.

Hair

Twist ends of each hair strand in opposite directions so that length of chain curls.
Sew centre of each of 10 strands of hair to top of head.

Hat tassel

Using 2.50mm (US size C-2) hook and A, make 6 ch and fasten off.
Sew tassel just made to top of hat, using one tail-end of yarn, then weave other tail-end into tassel.
Sew hat to top of doll's head, covering hair seam.

Scarf

Wrap scarf around doll's neck and sew in place.

Bag

Using D, make a bullion knot on right side at centre of last row on one bag piece.
Sew bag pieces together.
Sew bag handles to one of doll's hands.

ANNIE OVERBLOUSE

Annie thinks this little overblouse with its lovely textured stitch is just the thing to wear on an autumn day. Find a favourite button for it like Annie's, to make it look extra special.

BEFORE YOU BEGIN

SIZES AND MEASUREMENTS

To fit ages (in years)	2–3	3–4	4–5
To fit chest	56cm	61cm	66cm
	22in	24in	26in
Finished measurements			
Around chest	66cm	71cm	76cm
	26in	28in	30in
Length to shoulder	29cm	32cm	35cm
	11½in	12¾in	13¾in

YARN

Rowan *Pure Wool DK* (50g/1¾oz balls) as follows:

gold (Honey 033)	4 balls	4 balls	5 balls

HOOKS

3.00mm (US size D-3) crochet hook
3.50mm (US size E-4) crochet hook

EXTRAS

1 button 2cm/¾in in diameter

TENSION

20 sts and 24 rows to 10cm/4in measured over dc using 3.50mm (US size E-4) crochet hook or *size necessary to obtain correct tension.*

ABBREVIATIONS

See page 110.

GETTING STARTED

BACK

Using 3.00mm (US size D-3) hook, make 62 (67: 72) ch.

Foundation row (RS) Yrh and insert hook in 3rd ch from hook, yrh and draw a loop through ch and through first loop on hook, yrh and draw through rem 2 loops on hook, *yrh and insert hook in next ch, yrh and draw a loop through ch and through first loop on hook, yrh and draw through rem 2 loops on hook; rep from * to end, turn. 61 (66: 71) sts.

Row 1 (patt row) 2 ch (to count as first st), miss first st, *yrh and insert hook in next st, yrh and draw a loop through st and through first loop on hook, yrh and draw through rem 2 loops on hook; rep from * to end, working last st in 2nd of 2-ch, turn.

Rep last row 5 times more, ending with a RS row. Change to 3.50mm (US size E-4) hook.**

Next row (WS) 1 ch (does NOT count as a st), 1 dc in first st, *2 ch, miss next st, 1 dc in next st, 2 ch, miss next 2 sts, 1 dc in next st; rep from * to end, working last dc in 2nd of 2-ch, turn.

Beg main patt as follows:

Main patt row 1 (RS) 3 ch (to count as first tr), 1 tr in first dc, *3 tr in next dc; rep from * to last dc, 2 tr in last dc, turn. 23 (25: 27) 3-tr groups.

Main patt row 2 1 ch (does NOT count as a st), 1 dc in first tr, *2 ch, miss next 2 tr, 1 dc in next tr; rep from * to end, working last dc in 3rd of 3-ch, turn. (Last 2 rows form main patt when repeated.)

Work 9 (11: 13) rows more in patt, ending with a RS row.

Shape sleeves

Next row (WS) 1 ch (does NOT count as a st), 1 dc in first tr, [2 ch, miss 1 tr, 1 dc in next tr] 3 times, *2 ch, miss next 2 tr, 1 dc in next tr; rep from * to last 6 sts, [2 ch, miss 1 tr, 1 dc in next tr] 3 times, working last dc in 3rd of 3-ch, turn.

Next row 3 ch (to count as first tr), 1tr in first dc, *3 tr in next dc; rep from * to last dc, 2 tr in last dc, turn. (2 3-tr groups increased.)

Rep last 2 rows twice more.

Mark each end of last row with a coloured thread.

Work straight in patt for 16 (18: 20) rows. Fasten off.

FRONT

Work as given for Back to **.

Divide for front opening

Divide for front opening as follows:

1st and 3rd sizes only:

Next row (WS) 1 ch (does NOT count as a st), 1 dc in first st, [2 ch, miss next st, 1 dc in next st, 2 ch, miss next 2 sts, 1 dc in next st] 5 (—: 6) times, turn.

2nd size only:

Next row (WS) 1 ch (does NOT count as a st), 1 dc in first st, [2 ch, miss next st, 1 dc in next st, 2 ch, miss next 2 sts, 1 dc in next st] 5 times, 2 ch, miss next st, 1 dc in next st, turn.

All sizes:

Working on these sts only for right front, beg main patt as follows:

Main patt row 1 (RS) 3 ch (to count as first tr), 1 tr in first dc, *3 tr in next dc; rep from * to last dc, 2 tr in last dc, turn. 9 (10: 11) 3-tr groups.

Main patt row 2 1 ch (does NOT count as a st), 1 dc in first tr, *2 ch, miss next 2 tr, 1 dc in next tr; rep from * to end, working last dc in 3rd of 3-ch, turn.

(Last 2 rows form main patt when repeated.)
Work 6 (8: 10) rows more in patt, ending with a WS row.

Shape right front neck

Next row (dec row) (RS) 3 ch (to count as first tr), 1 tr in first dc, 1 tr in next dc, 1 tr in next 2-ch sp, 1 tr in next dc, *3 tr in next dc; rep from * to last dc, 2 tr in last dc, turn. *(1 tr group decreased at neck edge.)*
Work straight in patt for 2 rows, ending with a RS row.

Shape sleeve

Next row (WS) 1 ch (does NOT count as a st), 1 dc in first tr, [2 ch, miss 1 tr, 1 dc in next tr] 3 times, *2 ch, miss next 2 tr, 1 dc in next tr; rep from * to end, working last dc in 3rd of 3-ch, turn.

Next row 3 ch (to count as first tr), 1 tr in first dc, *3 tr in next dc; rep from * to last dc, 2 tr in last dc, turn. *(1 3-tr group increased.)*

Next row 1 ch (does NOT count as a st), 1 dc in first tr, [2 ch, miss 1 tr, 1 dc in next tr] 3 times,
*2 ch, miss next 2 tr, 1 dc in next tr; rep from * to end, working last dc in 3rd of 3-ch, turn.

Next row 3 ch (to count as first tr), 1 tr in first dc, 1 tr in next dc, 1 tr in next 2-ch sp, 1 tr in next dc, *3 tr in next dc; rep from * to last dc, 2 tr in last dc, turn. *(1 tr group decreased at neck edge.)*

Next row 1 ch (does NOT count as a st), 1 dc in first tr, [2 ch, miss 1 tr, 1 dc in next tr] 3 times, *2 ch, miss next 2 tr, 1 dc in next tr; rep from * to end, working last dc in 3rd of 3-ch, turn.

Next row 3 ch (to count as first tr), 1 tr in first dc, *3 tr in next dc; rep from * to last dc, 2 tr in last dc, turn.

Mark side-seam edge of last row with a coloured thread.

Work straight in patt for 3 rows, ending with a WS row.

Cont in patt, work neck decrease as set on next row and then on foll 6th row, ending with a RS row.

Work straight in patt for 6 (8: 10) rows (Front should now match same length as Back to shoulder).

Fasten off.

1st and 3rd sizes only:

With WS facing, miss centre 9 sts and rejoin yarn with a ss to next st, 1 dc in same place as ss, [2 ch, miss next st, 1 dc in next st, 2 ch, miss next 2 sts, 1 dc in next st] 5 (—: 6) times, working last dc in 2nd of 2-ch, turn.

2nd size only:

With WS facing, miss centre 9 sts and rejoin yarn with a ss to next st, 1 dc in same place as ss, 2 ch, miss next 2 sts, 1 dc in next st, [2 ch, miss next st, 1 dc in next st, 2 ch, miss next 2 sts, 1 dc in next st] 5 times, working last dc in 2nd of 2-ch, turn.

All sizes:

Beg main patt as follows:

Main patt row 1 (RS) 3 ch (to count as first tr), 1 tr in first dc, *3 tr in next dc; rep from * to last dc, 2 tr in last dc, turn. 9 (10: 11) 3-tr groups.

Main patt row 2 1 ch (does not count as a st), 1 dc in first tr, *2 ch, miss next 2 tr, 1 dc in next tr; rep from * to end, working last dc in 3rd of

3-ch, turn.

(Last 2 rows form main patt when repeated.)
Work 6 (8: 10) rows more in patt, ending with a WS row.

Shape left front neck

Next row (dec row) (RS) 3 ch (to count as first tr), 1 tr in first dc, *3 tr in next dc; rep from * to last 3 dc, 1 tr in next dc, 1 tr in next 2-ch sp, 1 tr in next dc, 2 tr in last dc, turn. *(1 tr group decreased at neck edge.)*
Work straight in patt for 2 rows, ending with a RS row.

Shape sleeve

Next row (WS) 1 ch (does NOT count as a st), 1 dc in first tr, *2 ch, miss next 2 tr, 1 dc in next tr; rep from * to last 6 sts, [2 ch, miss 1 tr, 1 dc in next tr] 3 times, working last dc in 3rd of 3-ch, turn.
Next row 3 ch (to count as first tr), 1 tr in first dc, *3 tr in next dc; rep from * to last dc, 2 tr in last dc, turn. *(1 3-tr group increased.)*
Next row 1 ch (does NOT count as a st), 1 dc in first tr, *2 ch, miss next 2 tr, 1 dc in next tr; rep from * to last 6 sts, [2 ch, miss 1 tr, 1 dc in next tr] 3 times, working last dc in 3rd of 3-ch, turn.
Next row 3 ch (to count as first tr), 1 tr in first dc, *3 tr in next dc; rep from * to last 3 dc, 1 tr in next dc, 1 tr in next 2-ch sp, 1 tr in next dc, 2 tr in last dc, turn. *(1 tr group decreased at neck edge.)*
Next row 1 ch (does NOT count as a st), 1 dc in first tr, *2 ch, miss next 2 tr, 1 dc in next tr; rep from * to last 6 sts, [2 ch, miss 1 tr, 1 dc in next tr] 3 times, working last dc in 3rd of 3-ch, turn.
Next row 3 ch (to count as first tr), 1 tr in first dc, *3 tr in next dc; rep from * to last dc, 2 tr in last dc, turn.
Mark side-seam edge of last row with a coloured thread.
Work straight in patt for 3 rows, ending with a WS row.
Cont in patt, work neck decrease as set on next row and then on foll 6th row, ending with a RS row.
Work straight in patt for 6 (8: 10) rows (Front should now match same length as Back to shoulder).
Fasten off.

TO FINISH

Press pieces lightly on wrong side, following instructions on yarn label.
Sew shoulder seams.
Sew side seams up to coloured markers.

Front band and neckband

With RS facing and using 3.00mm (US size D-3) hook, work edging along front opening edges and neck edge as follows:
Row 1 (RS) Join yarn with a ss to first row-end at bottom of right front opening, 2 ch, then working first dc in same place as ss, work 2 dc in each 'tr' row-end and 1 dc in each 'dc' at row-end up right front edge to shoulder, work 1 dc in each tr across back neck edge, then work 2 dc in each 'tr' row-end and 1 dc in each 'dc' row-end down left front edge, turn.
Row 2 2 ch, miss first dc, *yrh and insert hook in next dc, yrh and draw a loop through dc and through first loop on hook, yrh and draw through rem 2 loops on hook; rep from * to end, working last st in 2nd of 2-ch, turn.
Row 3 2 ch, miss first st, *yrh and insert hook in next st, yrh and draw a loop through st and through first loop on hook, yrh and draw through rem 2 loops on hook; rep from * to end, working last st in 2nd of 2-ch, turn.
Rep last row twice more.
Fasten off.

Sleeve edging

With RS facing, using 3.00mm (US size D-3) hook, work edging along sleeve edge as follows:
Round 1 (RS) Join yarn with a ss to first row-end on sleeve edge at side seam, then working first dc in same place as ss, work 2 dc in each 'tr' row-end and 1 dc in each 'dc' row-end all around armhole, join with a ss to first dc, do not turn.
Round 2 (RS) 2 ch, miss first dc, *yrh and insert hook in next dc, yrh and draw a loop through dc and through first loop on hook, yrh and draw through rem 2 loops on hook; rep from * to end, working last st in 2nd of 2-ch.
Fasten off.
Sew row-end edges of front bands to missed sts at centre front.
Sew on button.

COSY CONNIE JUMPER

See how lovely Connie looks in her Cosy Jumper with it's sweet three-quarter-length sleeves. The simple textured stitch is very pretty and really quite easy to work. Connie is happy to wear it all day long as it is so warm and comfortable, and orange is her favourite colour.

BEFORE YOU BEGIN

SIZES AND MEASUREMENTS

To fit ages (in years)	2–3	3–4	4–5
To fit chest	56cm	61cm	66cm
	22in	24in	26in
Finished measurements			
Around chest	66cm	71cm	76cm
	26in	28in	30in
Length to shoulder	37cm	39cm	41cm
	14½in	15½in	16in
Sleeve length	16cm	19cm	23cm
	6½in	7½in	9in

YARN

Rowan *Pure Wool DK* (50g/1¾ oz balls) as follows:

A	orange (Tangerine 040)	6 balls	7 balls	8 balls
B	light turquoise (Pier 003)	1 ball	1 ball	1 ball

HOOKS

3.50mm (US size E-4) crochet hook
4.00mm (US size G-6) crochet hook

EXTRAS

1 button 11mm/⁷⁄₁₆in in diameter

TENSION

20 sts and 24 rows to 10cm/4in measured over dc using 3.50mm (US size E-4) crochet hook *or size necessary to obtain correct tension.*

ABBREVIATIONS

dc2tog = [insert hook in next st, yrh and draw a loop through] twice, yrh and draw through all 3 loops on hook — *one st decreased.*
See also page 110.

UPPER BACK AND SLEEVES

Using 3.50mm (US size E-4) hook and A, make 67 (73: 79) ch.
Foundation row (RS) 1 dc in 2nd ch from hook, 1 dc in each of rem ch, turn. *66 (72: 78) dc.*
Row 1 (patt row) 1 ch (does NOT count as a st), 1 dc in each dc to end, turn.
(Last row forms simple dc patt when repeated.)
Cont in dc throughout, work 0 (2: 4) more rows, ending with a WS row.

Shape sleeves

Next row (RS) Make 4 (5: 6) ch, 1 dc in 2nd ch from hook, 1 dc in each of next 2 (3: 4) ch, 1 dc in each dc to end, turn.
Rep last row 5 times more, ending with a WS row. *84 (96: 108) dc.***
Work straight until Back measures 16 (18: 20) cm/6¼ (7: 7¾) in from beg, ending with a WS row.

Shape upper sleeve, shoulder and back neck

Next row (RS) 1 ss in each of first 8 (9: 10) dc, 1 ch, 1 dc in same dc as last ss, 1 dc in each dc to last 7 (8: 9) dc, turn. *70 (80: 90) dc.*
Next row 1 ss in each of first 8 (9: 10) dc, 1 ch, 1 dc in same dc as last ss, 1 dc in each of next 13 (16: 19) dc, work dc2tog over next 2 dc, 1 dc in next dc, turn. *16 (19: 22) dc.*
Working on these sts only for first side of neck, cont as follows:
Next row (RS) 1 ch, 1 dc in first dc, work dc2tog over next 2 dc, 1 dc in each of next 6 (8: 10) dc. *8 (10: 12) dc.*
Fasten off.
With WS facing, return to sts left unworked, miss centre 22 (24: 26) dc and rejoin A with a ss to next dc, 1 ch, 1 dc in same dc as ss, work dc2tog over next 2 dc, 1 dc in each of next 14 (17: 20) dc, turn. *16 (19: 22) dc.*
Next row 1 ss in each of first 8 (9: 10) dc, 1 ch, 1 dc in same dc as last ss, 1 dc in each of next 5 (7: 9) dc, work dc2tog over next 2 dc, 1 dc in last dc. *8 (10: 12) dc.* Fasten off.

UPPER FRONT AND SLEEVES

Work as for Back to **.
Work straight for 4 rows, ending with a WS row.

Divide for front opening
Next row (RS) 1 ch, 1 dc in each of first 41 (47: 53) dc, turn.
Working on these sts only for left side of front opening, cont as follows:
Work straight until Front measures 11 (13: 15) cm/ 4¼ (5: 6) in from beg, ending with a WS row.

Shape left front neck
Next row (RS) 1 ch, 1 dc in each of first 32 (37: 42) dc, work dc2tog over next 2 dc, 1 dc in next dc, turn. *34 (39: 44) dc.*
Next row 1 ch, 1 dc in first dc, work dc2tog over next 2 dc, 1 dc in each dc to end, turn.
Next row 1 ch, 1 dc in each dc to last 3 dc, work dc2tog over next 2 dc, 1 dc in last dc, turn.
Rep last 2 rows until 29 (34: 39) dc rem.
Work straight until Front measures 16 (18: 20) cm/ 6¼ (7: 7¾) in from beg (same as Back to shoulder), ending with a WS row.

Shape left shoulder
Next row 1 ss in each of first 8 (9: 10) dc, 1 ch, 1 dc in same dc as last ss, 1 dc in each dc to end, turn.
Next row 1 ch, 1 dc in each dc to last 7 (8: 9) dc, turn.
Next row 1 ss in each of first 8 (9: 10) dc, 1 ch, 1 dc in same dc as last ss, 1 dc in each dc to end. *8 (10: 12) dc.*
Fasten off.
With RS facing, return to sts left unworked, miss centre 2 dc and rejoin A with a ss to next dc, 1 ch, 1 dc in same place as ss, 1 dc in each dc to end, turn. *41 (47: 53) dc.*
Work straight until Front measures 11 (13: 15) cm/ 4¼ (5: 6) in from beg, ending with a WS row.

Shape right front neck
Next row (RS) 1 ss in each of first 7 (8: 9) dc, 1 ch, 1 dc in same place as last ss, work dc2tog over next 2 dc, 1 dc in each dc to end, turn. *34 (39: 44) dc.*
Next row 1 ch, 1 dc in each dc to last 3 dc, work dc2tog over next 2 dc, 1 dc in last dc, turn.

Next row 1 ch, 1 dc in first dc, work dc2tog over next 2 dc, 1 dc in each dc to end, turn.
Rep last 2 rows until 29 (34: 39) dc rem.
Work straight until Front measures 16 (18: 20) cm/ 6¼ (7: 7¾) in from beg (same as Back to shoulder), ending with a WS row.

Shape right shoulder
Next row (RS) 1 ch, 1 dc in each dc to last 7 (8: 9) dc, turn.
Next row 1 ss in each of first 8 (9: 10) dc, 1 ch, 1 dc in same dc as last ss, 1 dc in each dc to end, turn.
Next row 1 ch, 1 dc in each dc to last 7 (8: 9) dc, turn. *8 (10: 12) dc.*
Fasten off.

LOWER BACK

With RS facing and using 3.50mm (US size E-4) hook and A, work Lower Back along foundation-chain edge of Back as follows:
Foundation row (RS) Join A with a ss to first foundation ch, 1 ch, 1 dc in same place as ss, 1 dc in each of next 33 (36: 39) ch, 2 dc in next ch, 1 dc in each of rem ch. *67 (73: 79) dc.*
Patt row 1 2 ch, [1 dc, 1 tr, 1 htr] all in first dc, *miss next 2 dc, [1 dc, 1 tr, 1 htr] all in next dc; rep from * to end, turn.
Patt row 2 2 ch, *[1 dc, 1 tr, 1 htr] all in next dc; rep from * to end, 1 ss in 2nd of 2-ch, turn.
(Last row forms patt when repeated.)
Work in patt until work measures 23 (25: 27) cm/ 9 (9¾: 10½) in from shoulder.
Change to 4.00mm (US size G-6) hook.
Cont in patt until work measures 37 (39: 41) cm/ 14½ (15½: 16) in from shoulder, ending with a WS row.
Fasten off.

LOWER FRONT

Work Lower Front along foundation-chain edge of Front as for Lower Back.

LOWER SLEEVES (both alike)

Sew shoulder seams.
With RS facing and using 3.50mm (US size E-4) hook and A, work Lower Sleeve along row-end edge of end of sleeve as follows:
Foundation row (RS) Join A with a ss to first

row-end at end of sleeve, 1 ch, 1 dc in same place as ss, work 39 (45: 51) more dc evenly across row-ends. 40 *(46: 52) dc.*

Patt row 1 2 ch, [1 dc, 1 tr, 1 htr] all in first dc, *miss next 2 dc, [1 dc, 1 tr, 1 htr] all in next dc; rep from * to end, turn.

Patt row 2 2 ch, *[1 dc, 1 tr, 1 htr] all in next dc; rep from * to end, 1 ss in 2nd of 2-ch, turn.

(Last row forms patt when repeated.)

Cont in patt until Lower Sleeve measures 5 (6: 7) cm/2 (2½: 2¾) in.

Change to 4.00mm (US size G-6) hook.

Cont in patt for 6 (7: 8) cm/2½ (2¾: 3) in more, ending with a WS row.

Fasten off.

TO FINISH

Press pieces very lightly on wrong side, following instructions on yarn label.

Neck edging

With RS facing and using 3.50mm (US size E-4) hook and B, work neck edging as follows:

Round 1 (RS) Join B with a ss to neck edge at right shoulder seam, 1 ch, 1 dc in same place as ss, then work a row of dc evenly around neck edge, making a button loop of 6-ch 4 rows below neck edge on right front and working 2 dc in each corner at top of front opening and dc2tog at inner corners at base of front opening, join with a ss to first dc.

Fasten off.

Sew side and sleeve seams.

Sew on button to correspond with button loop.

BESSIE BIRD COAT

Warm, woolly, cosy, practical and fun, a Bessie Bird Coat is just what you need for playing outside in the winter. Keep it simple with just the colourful stripy belt or make it truely lovely by decorating the pockets with two Bessie Birds. Either way, it looks good and is extra snug worn with the Winter Warmer hat and scarf on page 92.

scarf on page 92.

See also page 110.

BEFORE YOU BEGIN

SIZES AND MEASUREMENTS

To fit ages (in years)	2–3	3–4	4–5
To fit chest	56cm	61cm	66cm
	22in	24in	26in
Finished measurements			
Around chest	63cm	68cm	73cm
	24¾ in	26¾ in	28¾ in
Length to shoulder	48cm	55cm	62cm
	19in	21¾ in	24½ in
Sleeve length	22 cm	25cm	28cm
	8½ in	10in	11in

YARN

Rowan *Pure Wool DK* (50g/1¾ oz balls) as follows:

A	red (Kiss 036)	8 balls	9 balls	10 balls
B	light turquoise (Pier 006)	1 ball	2 balls	2 balls
C	mid green (Parsley 020)	1 ball	1 ball	1 ball
D	yellow (Gilt 032)	1 ball	1 ball	1 ball

HOOK

3.50mm (US size E-4) crochet hook

EXTRAS FOR BELT AND BIRD MOTIFS

1 buckle (for optional belt)
2 ecru buttons 9mm/⅜in in diameter, for optional bird motifs

TENSION

25 sts and 21 rows to 10cm/4in measured over patt using 3.50mm (US size E-4) crochet hook or *size necessary to obtain correct tension.*

ABBREVIATIONS

dc2tog = [insert hook in next st, yrh and draw a loop through] twice, yrh and draw through all 3 loops on hook — *one st decreased.*
See also page 110.

GETTING STARTED

COAT

BACK

Using 3.50mm (US size E-4) hook and B, make 103 (113: 123) ch.
Fasten off.
Change to A on next row as follows:
Foundation row (RS) Join A with a ss to first ch, 1 ch (does NOT count as a st), 1 dc in same place as ss, 1 dc in next ch, *1 ch, miss 1 ch, 1 dc in next ch; rep from * to last ch, 1 dc in last ch, turn. *103 (113: 123) sts — counting each dc and each 1-ch sp as a st.*
Patt row 1 1 ch (does NOT count as a st), 1 dc in first dc, *1 ch, 1 dc in next 1-ch sp; rep from * to last 2 dc, 1 ch, 1 dc in last dc, turn.
Patt row 2 1 ch, 1 dc in first dc, *1 dc in next 1-ch sp, 1 ch; rep from * to last 1-ch sp, 1 dc in next 1-ch sp, 1 dc in last dc, turn.
(Last 2 rows form patt when repeated.)
Cont in patt as set throughout, work 7 (9: 11) rows more, ending with a WS row.
Next row (dec row) (RS) 1 ch, 1 dc in first dc, [1 dc in next 1-ch sp, 1 ch] 5 times, work dc2tog over next 2 ch sps, work in patt to last 7 ch sps, work dc2tog over next 2 ch sps, [1 ch, 1 dc in next 1-ch sp] 5 times, 1 dc in last dc, turn. *(4 sts decreased.)*
Work straight for 9 rows, ending with a WS row.
Rep last 10 rows 4 (5: 6) times more and then the dec row again. 79 *(85: 91)* sts.
Work straight until Back measures 35 (41: 47) cm/ 13¾ (16: 18½) in from beg, ending with a WS row.

Shape armholes

Next row (RS) 1 ss in each of first 3 sts, 1 ch, 1 dc in next 1-ch sp, work in patt to last 3 sts, turn. 73 *(79: 85)* sts.

Next row 1 ch, 1 dc in first dc, work dc2tog over next 2 ch sps, work in patt to last 2 ch sps, work dc2tog over next 2 ch sps, 1 dc in last dc, turn.

Next row 1 ch, 1 dc in first dc, 1 ch, work dc2tog over next 2 ch sps, work in patt to last 2 ch sps, work dc2tog over next 2 ch sps, 1 ch, 1 dc in last dc, turn.

Next row 1 ch, 1 dc in first dc, work dc2tog over next 2 ch sps, work in patt to last 2 ch sps, work dc2tog over next 2 ch sps, 1 dc in last dc, turn. 61 *(67: 73)* sts.

Work straight until Back measures 45 (52: 59) cm/ 17¾ (20½: 23¼) in from beg, ending with a WS row.

Shape back neck

Next row (RS) 1 ch, 1 dc in first dc, [1 ch, 1 dc in next 1-ch sp] 8 (9: 10) times, turn. 17 *(19: 21)* sts.
Working on these sts only for first side of neck, cont as follows:

Next row 1 ch, 1 dc in first dc, work dc2tog over next 2 ch sps, work in patt to end, turn.

Next row Work in patt to last 2 ch sps, work dc2tog over next 2 ch sps, 1 ch, 1 dc in last dc, turn. 13 *(15: 17)* sts.
Work straight for 3 rows.
Fasten off.

With RS facing, return to sts left unworked, miss centre 27 (29: 31) sts and rejoin A with a ss to next 1-ch sp, 1 ch, 1 dc in same place as ss, work in patt to end, turn. 17 *(19: 21)* sts.

Next row Work in patt to last 2 ch sps, work dc2tog over next 2 ch sps, 1 dc in last dc, turn.

Next row 1 ch, 1 dc in first dc, 1 ch, work dc2tog over next 2 ch sps, work in patt to end, turn. 13 *(15: 17)* sts.
Work straight for 3 rows.
Fasten off.

POCKET LININGS (make 2)

Using 3.50mm (US size E-4) hook and B, make 22 (24: 26) ch.

Foundation row (RS) 1 dc in 2nd ch from hook, 1 dc in next ch, *1 ch, miss 1 ch, 1 dc in next ch; rep from * to last ch, 1 dc in last ch, turn. 21 *(23: 25)* sts.

Patt row 1 1 ch (does NOT count as a st), 1 dc in first dc, *1 ch, 1 dc in next 1-ch sp; rep from * to last 2 dc, 1 ch, 1 dc in last dc, turn.

Patt row 2 1 ch, 1 dc in first dc, *1 dc in next 1-ch sp, 1 ch; rep from * to last 1-ch sp, 1 dc in next 1-ch sp, 1 dc in last dc, turn.
(Last 2 rows form patt when repeated.)
Cont in patt as set, work 11 (13: 15) rows more.
Fasten off.

LEFT FRONT

Using 3.50mm (US size E-4) hook and B, make 55 (61: 67) ch.
Fasten off.
Change to A on next row as follows:

Foundation row (RS) Join A with a ss to first ch, 1 ch (does NOT count as a st), 1 dc in same place as ss, 1 dc in next ch, *1 ch, miss 1 ch, 1 dc in next ch; rep from * to last ch, 1 dc in last ch, turn. 55 *(61: 67)* sts.

Patt row 1 1 ch (does NOT count as a st), 1 dc in first dc, *1 ch, 1 dc in next 1-ch sp; rep from * to last 2 dc, 1 ch, 1 dc in last dc, turn.

Patt row 2 1 ch, 1 dc in first dc, *1 dc in next 1-ch sp, 1 ch; rep from * to last 1-ch sp, 1 dc in next 1-ch sp, 1 dc in last dc, turn.
(Last 2 rows form patt when repeated.)
Cont in patt as set throughout, work 7 (9: 11) rows more, ending with a WS row.

Next row (dec row) (RS) 1 ch, 1 dc in first dc, [1 dc in next 1-ch sp, 1 ch] 5 times, work dc2tog over next 2 ch sps, work in patt to end, turn.
(2 sts decreased.)
Work straight for 9 rows, ending with a WS row.
Rep last 10 rows 2 (3: 4) times more and then the dec row again. 47 *(51: 55)* sts.
Work straight for 5 rows, ending with a WS row.

Place pocket lining

Next row (RS) 1 ch, 1 dc in first dc, [1 dc in next 1-ch sp, 1 ch] 8 (9: 10) times; then with RS of pocket lining facing WS of Front, work across pocket lining as follows – miss first dc, 1 dc in next 1-ch sp, [1 ch, 1 dc in next 1-ch sp] 9 (10: 11) times; miss 19 (21: 23) sts of Front, work in patt to end, turn. 47 *(51: 55)* sts.

Work straight for 3 rows, ending with a WS row.
Next row (RS) 1 ch, 1 dc in first dc, [1 dc in next 1-ch sp, 1 ch] 5 times, work dc2tog over next 2 ch sps, work in patt to end, turn. *45 (49: 53) sts.*
Work straight for 9 rows, ending with a WS row.
Next row (RS) 1 ch, 1 dc in first dc, [1 dc in next 1-ch sp, 1 ch] 5 times, work dc2tog over next 2 ch sps, work in patt to end, turn. *43 (47: 51) sts.*
Work straight until Left Front measures 35 (41: 47) cm/13¾ (16: 18½) in from beg (same as Back to armhole), ending with a WS row.

Shape armhole
Next row (RS) 1 ss in each of first 3 sts, 1 ch, 1 dc in next 1-ch sp, work in patt to end. *40 (44: 48) sts.*
Next row Work in patt to last 2 ch sps, work dc2tog over next 2 ch sps, 1 dc in last dc, turn.
Next row 1 ch, 1 dc in first dc, 1 ch, work dc2tog over next 2 ch sps, work in patt to end, turn.
Next row Work in patt to last 2 ch sps, work dc2tog over next 2 ch sps, 1 dc in last dc, turn. *34 (38: 42) sts.*
Work straight until Left Front measures 40 (47: 54) cm/15¾ (18½: 21¼) in from beg, ending with a WS row.

Shape neck
Next row 1 ch, 1 dc in first dc, [1 ch, 1 dc in next 1-ch sp] 10 (11: 12) times, turn.
Next row 1 ch, 1 dc in first dc, work dc2tog over next 2 ch sps, work in patt to end, turn.
Next row Work in patt to last 2 ch sps, work dc2tog over next 2 ch sps, 1 ch, 1 dc in last dc, turn.
Rep last 2 rows once more. *13 (15: 17) sts.*
Work straight until Left Front measures same as Back to shoulder.
Fasten off.

RIGHT FRONT
Using 3.50mm (US size E-4) hook and B, make 55 (61: 67) ch.
Fasten off.
Change to A on next row as follows:
Foundation row (RS) Join A with a ss to first ch, 1 ch (does NOT count as a st), 1 dc in same place as ss, 1 dc in next ch, *1 ch, miss 1 ch, 1 dc in next ch; rep from * to last ch, 1 dc in last ch, turn. *55 (61: 67) sts.*
Patt row 1 1 ch (does NOT count as a st), 1 dc in first dc, *1 ch, 1 dc in next 1-ch sp; rep from * to last 2 dc, 1 ch, 1 dc in last dc, turn.
Patt row 2 1 ch, 1 dc in first dc, *1 ch, 1 dc in next 1-ch sp, 1 ch; rep from * to last 1-ch sp, 1 dc in next 1-ch sp, 1 dc in last dc, turn.
(Last 2 rows form patt when repeated.)
Cont in patt as set throughout, work 7 (9: 11) rows more, ending with a WS row.
Next row (dec row) (RS) Work in patt to last 7 ch sps, work dc2tog over next 2 ch sps, [1 ch, 1 dc in next 1-ch sp] 5 times, 1 dc in last dc, turn. *(2 sts decreased.)*
Work straight for 9 rows, ending with a WS row.
Rep last 10 rows 2 (3: 4) times more and then the dec row again. *47 (51: 55) sts.*
Work straight for 5 rows, ending with a WS row.

Place pocket lining
Next row (RS) 1 ch, 1 dc in first dc, [1 dc in next 1-ch sp, 1 ch] 5 times; then with RS of pocket lining facing WS of Front, work across pocket lining as follows — miss first dc, 1 dc in next 1-ch sp, [1 ch, 1 dc in next 1-ch sp] 9 (10: 11) times; miss 19 (21: 23) sts of Front, work in patt to end, turn. *47 (51: 55) sts.*
Work straight for 3 rows, ending with a WS row.
Next row (RS) Work in patt to last 7 ch sps, work dc2tog over next 2 ch sps, [1 ch, 1 dc in next 1-ch sp] 5 times, 1 dc in last dc, turn. *45 (49: 53) sts.*
Work straight for 9 rows, ending with a WS row.
Next row (RS) Work in patt to last 7 ch sps, work dc2tog over next 2 ch sps, [1 ch, 1 dc in next 1-ch sp] 5 times, 1 dc in last dc, turn. *43 (47: 51) sts.*
Work straight until Right Front measures 35 (41: 47) cm/13¾ (16: 18½) in from beg (same as Back to armhole), ending with a WS row.

Shape armhole
Next row (RS) Work in patt to last 3 sts, turn. *40 (44: 48) sts.*
Next row 1 ch, 1 dc in first dc, work dc2tog over next 2 ch sps, work in patt to end, turn.
Next row Work in patt to last 2 ch sps, work

dc2tog over next 2 ch sps, 1 ch, 1 dc in last dc, turn.

Next row 1 ch, 1 dc in first dc, work dc2tog over next 2 ch sps, work in patt to end, turn. *34 (38: 42) sts.*

Work straight until Right Front measures 40 (47: 54) cm/15¾ (18½: 21¼) in from beg, ending with a WS row.

Shape neck

Next row (RS) 1 ss in each of first 13 (15: 17) sts, 1 ch, 1 dc in next 1-ch sp, work in patt to end, turn.

Next row Work in patt to last 2 ch sps, work dc2tog over next 2 ch sps, 1 dc in last dc, turn.

Next row 1 ch, 1 dc in first dc, 1 ch, work dc2tog over next 2 ch sps, work in patt to end, turn.

Rep last 2 rows once more. *13 (15: 17) sts.*

Work straight until Right Front measures same as Back to shoulder.

Fasten off.

SLEEVES (make 2)

Using 3.50mm (US size E-4) hook and B, make 43 (47: 51) ch.

Fasten off.

Change to A on next row as follows:

Foundation row (RS) Join A with a ss to first ch, 1 ch (does NOT count as a st), 1 dc in same place as ss, 1 dc in next ch, *1 ch, miss 1 ch, 1 dc in next ch; rep from * to last ch, 1 dc in last ch, turn. *43 (47: 51) sts.*

Patt row 1 1 ch (does NOT count as a st), 1 dc in first dc, *1 ch, 1 dc in next ch sp; rep from * to last 2 dc, 1 ch, 1 dc in last dc, turn.

Patt row 2 1 ch, 1 dc in first dc, *1 dc in next 1-ch sp, 1 ch; rep from * to last 1-ch sp, 1 dc in next 1-ch sp, 1 dc in last dc, turn.

(Last 2 rows form patt when repeated.)

Cont in patt as set throughout, work 1 row more.

Next row (inc row) (RS) 1 ch, 1 dc in first dc, [1 dc in next 1-ch sp, 1 ch] 4 times, [1 dc, 1 ch, 1 dc] all in next 1-ch sp, work in patt to last 5 ch sps, [1 dc, 1 ch, 1 dc] all in next 1-ch sp, [1 ch, 1 dc in next 1-ch sp] 5 times, 1 dc in last dc. *(4 sts increased.)*

Work straight for 5 rows, ending with a WS row.

Rep last 6 rows 5 (6: 7) times more and then the inc row again. *71 (79: 87) sts.*

Work straight until Sleeve measures 22 (25: 28) cm/8½ (10: 11) in from beg, ending with a WS row.

Shape top of sleeve

Next row 1 ss in each of first 3 sts, 1 ch, 1 dc in next 1-ch sp, work in patt to last 3 sts, turn. *65 (73: 81) sts.*

Next row 1 ch, 1 dc in first dc, work dc2tog over next 2 ch sps, work in patt to last 2 ch sps, work dc2tog over next 2 ch sps, 1 dc in last dc, turn.

Next row 1 ch, 1 dc in first dc, 1 ch, work dc2tog over next 2 ch sps, work in patt to last 2 ch sps, work dc2tog over next 2 ch sps, 1 ch, 1 dc in last dc, turn.

Next row 1 ch, 1 dc in first dc, work dc2tog over next 2 ch sps, work in patt to last 2 ch sps, work dc2tog over next 2 ch sps, 1 dc in last dc, turn. *53 (61: 69) sts.*

Fasten off.

TO FINISH

Press pieces lightly on wrong side, following instructions on yarn label.

Sew shoulder seams.

Sew side seams. Sew sleeve seams and set in sleeves.

Sew pocket linings to wrong side of coat if bird motifs are not being made.

Edging

With RS facing and using 3.50mm (US size E-4) hook and B, work edging around edge of coat as follows:

Round 1 (RS) Join B with a ss to first row-end of Right Front at bottom edge of coat, then working up front edge, work 1 ch, 1 dc in same place as ss, 1 ch, miss first row-end, *1 dc in next row-end, 1 ch,* rep from * to * to corner at neck edge, work [1 dc, 1 ch, 1 dc] all into corner, cont working 1 ch and 1 dc alternately around neck edge to next corner, work [1 dc, 1 ch, 1 dc] all into corner, work down Left Front in patt as set to corner, then working into other side of foundation ch, work [1 ch, 1 dc in next 1-ch sp] all along bottom edge of coat to beg of round, join with a ss in first dc.

Do not turn work and do not fasten off.

Mark position for two buttonholes, 3cm/1¼in
and 10cm/4in from neck edge on Right Front,
then cont edging up Right Front as follows:
Next row (RS) 1 dc in first 1-ch sp, **1 ch, 1 dc in
next 1-ch sp,** rep from ** to ** to position of
first buttonhole, 3 ch, miss [1 dc, 1 ch and 1 dc],
1 dc in next 1-ch sp, rep from ** to ** to position
of second buttonhole, 3 ch, miss [1 dc, 1 ch and
1 dc], 1 dc in next 1-ch sp, cont in patt as set to
corner at neck edge, work [1 dc, 1 ch, 1 dc] all in
corner 1-ch sp, cont in patt to next corner, work
[1 dc, 1 ch, 1 dc] all in corner 1-ch sp, cont in
patt to bottom of Left Front.
Fasten off.

BUTTONS (make 2)

Using 3.50mm (US size E-4) hook and A, make 2
ch, leaving a long tail-end of yarn.
Round 1 (RS) 6 dc in 2nd ch from hook (working
over tail-end of yarn), join with a ss to first dc.
(Do not turn work, but work with RS always
facing.)
Round 2 1 ch (does NOT count as a st), 1 dc in
each dc to end, join with a ss to first dc. 6 dc.
Round 3 1 ch, work dc2tog over first dc (same
place as ss) and next dc, [work dc2tog over

next 2 dc] twice, join with a ss to first dc. 3 dc.
Fasten off, leaving a long tail-end of yarn.
Pull long tail-end of yarn inside first round of sts
to close ring, then thread tail-end into centre of
button and use it to stuff button.
Use other tail-end to sew buttons to edge of
Left Front to correspond with buttonholes.

BELT (optional)

TO MAKE BELT

The belt is made in two halves, that are joined
together lengthways along the centre.

First half
Using 3.50mm (US size E-4) hook and B, make
160 (165: 170) ch.
Fasten off, leaving a long tail-end of yarn.
Foundation row (RS) Using D, join yarn with a ss
to first ch, 1 ch (does NOT count as a st), 1 dc in
same place as ss, 1 dc in each of rem
ch, turn. 160 (165: 170) dc.
Fasten off.
Row 1 Using C, join yarn
with a ss to first dc, 1 ch
(does NOT count as a
st), 1 dc in same place
as ss, 1 dc in each dc
to end.
Fasten off.

Second half

Work second half in same way as first half, but turn work at end of row 1 and do not fasten off C.

Place first half behind second half with right sides of strips together and tops of last rows aligned, then still using C, join strips by working a row of dc through both pieces at once. Fasten off.

Edging at ends of belt

Using long tail-end of B, work a row of dc along each short end.
Fasten off.

BELT CARRIERS (make 3)

Using 3.50mm (US size E-4) hook and A, make 7 ch.

Foundation row (RS) 1 dc in 2nd ch from hook, 1 dc in each of rem ch, turn. 6 dc.

Row 1 1 ch (does not count as a st), 1 dc in each dc to end.
Fasten off.

TO FINISH

Press pieces lightly on wrong side, following instructions on yarn label.
Sew buckle to one end of belt.
Sew one belt carrier to each side seam and one to centre back. Thread belt through carriers.

BIRD MOTIFS (optional)

BIRDS' BODIES Ⓐ (make 2)

Using 3.50mm (US size E-4) hook and C, make 13 ch.

Foundation row (RS) 1 dc in 2nd ch from hook, 1 dc in each of rem ch, turn. 12 dc.

Row 1 (patt row) 1 ch (does NOT count as a st), 1 dc in each dc to end, turn.

(Last row forms simple dc patt when repeated.)
Cont in dc throughout, work 3 rows more.

Next row (dec row) 1 ch, 1 dc in first dc, work dc2tog over next 2 dc, 1 dc in each dc to last 3 dc, work dc2tog over next 2 dc, 1 dc in last dc, turn.

Work straight for 1 row.
Rep dec row twice. 6 dc.

Next row 1 ch, 1 dc in first dc, [work dc2tog

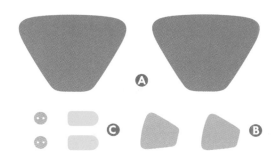

over next 2 dc] twice, 1 dc in last dc. 4 dc.
Fasten off.

WINGS Ⓑ (make 2)

Using 3.50mm (US size E-4) hook and B, make 5 ch.

Foundation row (RS) 1 dc in 2nd ch from hook, 1 dc in each of rem ch, turn. 4 dc.

Row 1 1 ch (does NOT count as a st), 1 dc in each dc to end, turn.

Row 2 1 ch, [work dc2tog over next 2 dc] twice, turn. 2 dc.

Row 3 1 ch, 1 dc in each of 2 dc.
Fasten off.

BEAKS Ⓒ (make 2)

Using 3.50mm (US size E-4) hook and D, make 4 ch.

Foundation row (RS) 1 dc in 2nd ch from hook, 1 dc in each of rem 2 ch. 3 dc.
Fasten off.

TO FINISH

Press pieces lightly on wrong side, following instructions on yarn label.

Using a blunt-ended yarn needle, embroider each bird body with two French knots in B and two in D as shown (see page 76).

Sew a beak and a wing to each bird, then sew on a button for the eye.

Sew one bird to front of each pocket, leaving beaks free.

Using B, embroider two legs below bird as shown. Using D, work three short straight stitches fanning out from bird for tail, then work a French knot in B at the end of each stitch.

Sew pocket linings to wrong side of coat.

MILO OWL JUMPER

Boys will love this sturdy little jumper with its simple stripy sleeves, simple embroidery and, of course, Milo. It is very easily made in double crochet and is ideal for keeping warm all winter. Try wearing it with the Winter Warmer scarf on page 93 – so cosy!

Try wearing it with the Winter Warmer scarf on page 93 – so cosy!

BEFORE YOU BEGIN

SIZES AND MEASUREMENTS

To fit ages in years	2–3	3–4	4–5
To fit chest	56cm	61cm	66cm
	22in	24in	26in
Finished measurements			
Around chest	74cm	79cm	84cm
	29in	31in	33in
Length to shoulder	37cm	39cm	41cm
	14½in	15¼in	16in
Sleeve length	21cm	26cm	29cm
	8¼in	10¼in	11½in

YARN

Rowan *Pure Wool DK* (50g/1¾ oz balls) as follows:

A	dark grey (Anthracite 003)	6 balls	7 balls	8 balls
B	mid green (Parsley 020)	1 ball	2 balls	2 balls
C	light turquoise (Pier 006)	1 ball	2 balls	2 balls

HOOK

3.50mm (US size E-4) crochet hook

EXTRAS

2 red buttons 11mm/⁷⁄₁₆in in diameter, for owl's eyes

TENSION

20 sts and 24 rows to 10cm/4in measured over dc using 3.50mm (US size E-4) crochet hook *or size necessary to obtain correct tension.*

ABBREVIATIONS

dc2tog = [insert hook in next st, yrh and draw a loop through] twice, yrh and draw through all 3 loops on hook – *one st decreased.*
See also page 110.

See also page 110.

GETTING STARTED

JUMPER

BACK

Using 3.50mm (US size E-4) hook and A, make 75 (80: 85) ch.

Foundation row (RS) 1 dc in 2nd ch from hook, 1 dc in each of rem ch, turn. *74 (79: 84) dc.*

Row 1 (patt row) 1 ch (does NOT count as a st), 1 dc in each dc to end, turn.
(Last row forms simple dc patt when repeated.)
Work 1 (3: 5) rows more in dc.
Cont in dc throughout, work 1 row in B, then 1 row in C.
Cut off B and C.
Cont in A, work until Back measures 22 (23: 24) cm/8¾ (9: 9½) in from beg, ending with a WS row.

Shape armholes

Next row (RS) 1 ss in each of first 6 (7: 8) dc, 1 ch, 1 dc same place as last ss, 1 dc in each dc to last 5 (6: 7) dc, turn. *64 (67: 70) dc.*

Next row 1 ch, 1 dc in first dc, work dc2tog over next 2 dc, 1 dc in each dc to last 3 dc, work dc2tog over next 2 dc, 1 dc in last dc, turn.
Rep last row twice more, ending with a WS row. *58 (61: 64) dc.***
Work straight until Back measures 36 (38: 40) cm/14 (15: 15¾) in from beg, ending with a WS row.

Shape back neck

Next row (RS) 1 ch, 1 dc in each of first 15 (16: 17) dc, work dc2tog over next 2 dc, 1 dc in next dc, turn. *17 (18: 19) dc.*

Working on these sts only for first side of neck, cont as follows:

Next row 1 ch, 1 dc in first dc, work dc2tog over next 2 dc, 1 dc in each dc to end, turn. *16 (17: 18) dc.*

Next row 1 ch, 1 dc in each dc to last 3 dc, work dc2tog over next 2 dc, 1 dc in last dc. *15 (16: 17) dc.*

Fasten off.

With RS facing, return to sts left unworked, miss centre 22 (23: 24) dc and rejoin A with a ss to next dc, 1 ch, 1 dc in same place as ss, work dc2tog over next 2 dc, 1 dc in each dc to end, turn. *17 (18: 19) dc.*

Next row 1 ch, 1 dc in each dc to last 3 dc, work dc2tog over next 2 dc, 1 dc in last dc, turn. *16 (17: 18) dc.*

Next row 1 ch, 1 dc in first dc, work dc2tog over next 2 dc, 1 dc in each dc to end. *15 (16: 17) dc.*
Fasten off.

FRONT

Work as for Back to **.
Work straight for 8 rows, ending with a WS row.

Shape front neck

Next row (RS) 1 ch, 1 dc in each of first 23 (24: 25) dc, work dc2tog over next 2 dc, 1 dc in next dc, turn. *25 (26: 27) dc.*

Working on these sts only for first side of neck, cont as follows:

Next row 1 ch, 1 dc in each dc to end, turn.

Next row 1 ch, 1 dc in each dc to last 3 dc, work dc2tog over next 2 dc, 1 dc in last dc, turn.

Rep last 2 rows until 15 (16: 17) dc rem.

Work straight until Front measures same as Back to shoulder.

Fasten off.

With RS facing, return to sts left unworked, miss centre 6 (7: 8) dc and rejoin A with a ss to next dc, 1 ch, 1 dc in same place as ss, work dc2tog over next 2 dc, 1 dc in each dc to end, turn. *25 (26: 27) dc.*

Next row 1 ch, 1 dc in each dc to end, turn.

Next row 1 ch, 1 dc in first dc, work dc2tog over next 2 dc, 1 dc in each dc to end, turn.

Rep last 2 rows until 15 (16: 17) dc rem.

Work straight until Front measures same as Back to shoulder.

Fasten off.

SLEEVES (make 2)

Using 3.50mm (US size E-4) hook and A, make 37 (39: 41) ch.

Foundation row (RS) 1 dc in 2nd ch from hook, 1 dc in each of rem ch, turn. *36 (38: 40) dc.*

Row 1 (patt row) 1 ch (does NOT count as a st), 1 dc in each dc to end, turn.

(Last row forms simple dc patt when repeated.)
Work 1 row more in dc.

Cont in dc throughout, work 1 row in B, then 1 row in C.

Cont in stripe sequence of [3 rows A, 3 rows B, 3 rows C] repeated throughout *and at the same time* shape Sleeve as follows:

Work 1 row.

Next row (inc row) (RS) 1 ch, 1 dc in each of first 4 dc, 2 dc in next dc, 1 dc in each dc to last 5 dc, 2 dc in next dc, 1 dc in each of last 4 dc, turn. *(2 dc increased.)*

Work straight for 3 rows.

Rep last 4 rows 9 (11: 12) times more and then the inc row again. *58 (64: 68) dc.*

Work straight for 3 (7: 11) rows, ending with 3 (3: 2) rows C (A: A).

Mark each end of last row with a coloured thread.

Work straight for 6 (7: 8) rows more.

Shape top of sleeve

Next row 1 ch, 1 dc in first dc, work dc2tog over next 2 dc, 1 dc in each dc to last 3 dc, work dc2tog over next 2 dc, 1 dc in last dc, turn.

Rep last row twice more. *52 (58: 62) dc.*
Fasten off.

TO FINISH

Press pieces lightly on wrong side, following instructions on yarn label.
Sew shoulder seams.

Neck edging

With RS facing and using 3.50mm (US size E-4) hook, work edging along neck as follows:

Round 1 (RS) Using A, join yarn with a ss to neck edge at right shoulder seam, 1 ch, 1 dc in same place as ss, then work a round of dc evenly around neck edge, join with a ss to first dc.
Fasten off.

Turn work and with WS facing, join in B on next round as follows:

Round 2 (WS) Using B, join yarn with a ss to last dc at end of last round, 1 ch, 1 dc in same place as ss, 1 dc in each dc to end of round, join with a ss to first dc.

Fasten off.

Turn work and with RS facing, join in C on next round as follows:

Round 3 (RS) Using C, join yarn with a ss to last dc at end of last round, 1 ch, 1 dc in same place as ss, 1 dc in each dc to 1 dc before first of two corners on centre front neck, work dc2tog over next 2 dc (to shape corner), 1 dc in each dc to 1 dc before second corner, work dc2tog over next 2 dc, 1 dc in each dc to end of round, join with a ss to first dc.

Fasten off.

Sew sleeves to armholes, stitching rows above coloured markers to armhole shaping on Front and Back. Sew side and sleeve seams.

Embroidery

Using a blunt-ended yarn needle and B, embroider a cross stitch over every alt dc all around jumper, one row up from stripe in C at lower edge.

On Front, miss one row of dc above row of cross stitches and embroider four cross stitches in same way above centre four cross stitches below, then miss one row of dc and embroider three cross stitches centred above last four.

OWL MOTIF

OWL'S BODY Ⓐ

Using 3.50mm (US size E-4) hook and C, make 9 ch.

Foundation row (RS) 1 dc in 2nd ch from hook, 1 dc in each of rem ch, turn. *8 dc.*

Row 1 (patt row) 1 ch (does NOT count as a st), 1 dc in each dc to end, turn.

(Last forms simple dc patt when repeated.)

Row 2 1 ch, 1 dc in first dc, 2 dc in next dc, 1 dc in each of next 4 dc, 2 dc in next dc, 1 dc in last dc, turn. *10 dc.*

Row 3 Rep row 1.

Row 4 1 ch, 1 dc in first dc, 2 dc in next dc, 1 dc in each of next 6 dc, 2 dc in next dc, 1 dc in last dc, turn. *12 dc.*

Cont in dc throughout, work straight for 7 rows, ending with a WS row.

Next row (dec row) (RS) 1 ch, 1 dc in first dc,

work dc2tog over next 2 dc, 1 dc in each dc to last 3 dc, work dc2tog over next 2 dc, 1 dc in last dc, turn. *10 dc.*

Rep last row twice more. *6 dc.*

Shape ears

Next row (WS) 1 ch, 1 dc in each of first 2 dc, turn. *2 dc.*

Working on these sts only for first ear, cont as follows:

**Next row 1 ch, 1 dc in each dc to end, turn.

Next row 1 ch, work dc2tog over first 2 dc. *1 dc.* Fasten off.**

With WS facing, miss centre 2 dc and rejoin C with a ss to next dc, 1 ch, 1 dc in same place as ss, 1 dc in last dc, turn. *2 dc.*

Complete as for first ear from ** to **.

OWL'S WINGS Ⓑ (make 2)

Using 3.50mm (US size E-4) hook and C, make 6 ch.

Round 1 (RS) 1 dc in 2nd ch from hook, 1 dc in each of next 4 ch, then working along other side of foundation ch, work 1 dc in each of next 5 ch, 4 tr in same place as last dc, 1 ss in same place as 4 tr.

Fasten off.

OWL'S BEAK Ⓒ

Using 3.50mm (US size E-4) hook and A, make 5 ch.

Foundation row (RS) 1 dc in 2nd ch from hook, 1 dc in each of rem 3 ch. *4 dc.*

Fasten off, leaving a long tail-end of yarn.

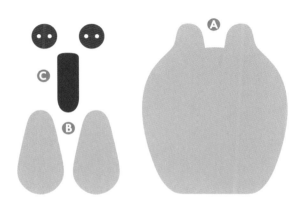

TO FINISH

Press pieces lightly on wrong side, following instructions on yarn label.

Wings, eyes and beak

With 4-tr group at bottom of wing, sew top of one side of each wing to owl's body as shown (see page 86).
For eyes, sew on two buttons as shown, using A. Sew one end of beak to owl's body between eyes.

Embroidery

Using a blunt-ended yarn needle, work embroidery as follows:
Using B, sew two vertical straight stitches at centre of each ear.
Using A, sew three straight stitches fanning out downwards from the same point to form feet at lower end of owl's body.

Using B, embroider four cross stitches across centre of owl's body, leaving one dc free between them (position them six rows up from lower edge, and over two rows vertically and 1 dc horizontally).
Miss a row of dc and using B, work three smaller cross stitches (over only one row vertically) below the first four.
Using A, work a short horizontal stitch across centre of each cross stitch.
Leaving wings and ears free, sew owl to jumper above cross stitches at centre of Front.

WINTER WARMERS

Boys and girls can play outside all day long when they are wearing their Winter Warmers! Easily made, the hat is snug with cosy earflaps and the scarf is superbly warm as it is folded to make it double thickness. Enjoy the winter weather!

BEFORE YOU BEGIN

SIZES AND MEASUREMENTS

To fit ages (in years)	2–3	3–4	4–5
Finished hat measurements			
Circumference	44cm	46cm	48cm
	17½in	18in	19in
Length from centre top, excluding flaps	17cm	18.5cm	20cm
	6½in	7¼in	8in

Scarf size
The finished scarf measures 15cm/6in by 70cm/27½in.

YARN

Rowan *Pure Wool DK* (50g/1¾ oz balls) as follows:

Girl's Hat and Scarf

A	red (Kiss 036)	2 balls	2 balls	2 balls
B	light turquoise (Pier 006)	1 ball	1 ball	1 ball
C	mid green (Parsley 020)	1 ball	1 ball	1 ball

Boy's Hat and Scarf

A	dark grey (Anthracite 003)	1 ball	1 ball	1 ball
B	light turquoise (Pier 006)	1 ball	1 ball	1 ball
C	mid green (Parsley 020)	1 ball	1 ball	1 ball

Note: If you are making only either the hat or the scarf, you will need only one ball of each of the three colours.

HOOK
4.00mm (US size G-6) crochet hook

EXTRAS FOR SCARF
2 large poppers
1 button 22mm/⅞in in diameter

TENSION
16½ sts and 22 rows to 10cm/4in measured over dc using 4.00mm (US size G-6) crochet hook or *size necessary to obtain correct tension.*

ABBREVIATIONS
dc2tog = [insert hook in next st, yrh and draw a loop through] twice, yrh and draw through all 3 loops on hook — *one st decreased.*
See also page 110.

GETTING STARTED

HAT

TO MAKE HAT
The hat is worked starting at the top.
Using 4.00mm (US size G-6) hook and A, make 17 ch.
Foundation round (WS) Using A, 1 dc in 2nd ch from hook, 1 dc in each ch to last ch, 2 dc in last ch, then working along other side of foundation ch, miss first ch, 1 dc in each ch to end of this side of foundation ch, change to B and join with a ss to first ch, turn. *32 dc.*
(Remember to turn the work at the end of each round.)
Round 1 (RS) Using B, 1 ch (does NOT count as a st), 2 dc in first dc, 1 dc in each of next 14 dc, 2 dc in each of next 2 dc, 1 dc in each of next 14 dc, 2 dc in last dc, change to C and join with a ss to first ch, turn. *36 dc.*
Round 2 Using C, 1 ch, 2 dc in first dc, 1 dc in each of next 16 dc, 2 dc in each of next 2 dc, 1 dc in each of next 16 dc, 2 dc in last dc, change to A and join with a ss to first ch, turn. *40 dc.*
Round 3 Using A, 1 ch, 2 dc in first dc, 1 dc in each of next 18 dc, 2 dc in each of next 2 dc, 1 dc in each of next 18 dc, 2 dc in last dc, join with a ss to first ch, turn. *44 dc.*
Round 4 Using A, 1 ch, 2 dc in first dc, 1 dc in each of next 20 dc, 2 dc in each of next 2 dc, 1 dc in each of next 20 dc, 2 dc in last dc, change to B and join with a ss to first ch, turn. *48 dc.*
These 4 rounds form the stripe sequence of [1 row B, 1 row C, 2 rows A] repeated and set the positions for the increases.
Cont as now set with stripe sequence and increases (increasing 4 sts in each round) for

4 rounds more. 64 dc.

Keeping stripe sequence correct as set throughout, cont as follows:

Next round (patt round) Using correct colour, 1 ch (does NOT count as a st), 1 dc in each dc to to end of round, then using correct colour join with a ss to first ch, turn.

Increase as set on next round and then on foll alt round 1 (2: 3) times. 72 (76: 80) dc.

Rep patt round until hat measures 17 (18.5: 20) cm/6½ (7¼: 8) in from foundation ch, ending with 2 rounds in A and a WS row.

Fasten off.

Cut off B and C.

First earflap

With RS facing and using 4.00mm (US size G-6) hook and A, beg first earflap on next row as follows:

Next row (RS) Miss first 26 (27: 28) dc after fasten-off point and rejoin A with a ss to next dc, 1 ch, 1 dc in same place as ss, 1 dc in each of next 10 (11: 12) dc, turn. 11 (12: 13) dc.

Working on these sts only for first earflap, cont as follows:

**Next row 1 ch, 1 dc in each dc to end, turn.

Rep last row 3 (5: 7) times more.

Next row 1 ch, 1 dc in first dc, work dc2tog over next 2 dc, 1 dc in each dc to last 3 dc, work dc2tog over next 2 dc, 1 dc in last dc, turn.

Next row 1 ch, 1 dc in each dc to end, turn.

Rep last 2 rows twice more. 5 (6: 7) dc.

Next row 1 ch, work dc2tog over first 2 dc, 1 dc in each of next 1 (2: 3) dc, work dc2tog over last

2 dc. 3 *(4: 5)* dc.
Fasten off.**

Second earflap
With RS facing and using 4.00mm (US size G-6)
hook and A, beg second earflap on next row
as follows:

Next row (RS) Miss 24 *(25: 26)* dc after last
earflap and rejoin A with a ss to next dc, 1 ch,
1 dc in same place as ss, 1 dc in each of next
10 *(11: 12)* dc, turn. *11 (12: 13) dc.*
Working on these sts only for second earflap,
work as for first earflap from ** to **.

TO FINISH
Press lightly on wrong side, following instructions
on yarn label.

Edging
With RS facing and using 4.00mm (US size G-6)
hook and B, join yarn with a ss to a dc at centre
back of hat, 1 ch, 1 dc in same place as ss, then
work a row of dc evenly all around outside
edge of hat, join with a ss to first dc.
Fasten off.

SCARF

TO MAKE SCARF
Using 4.00mm (US size G-6) hook and A, make
95 ch.
Foundation round (WS) 1 ch, 1 dc in 2nd ch
from hook, 1 dc in each dc to last ch, 2 dc in last
ch, then working along other side of foundation
ch, miss first ch, 1 dc in each ch to end of this
side of foundation ch, change to B and join with
a ss to first ch, turn. *188 dc.*
(Remember to turn the work at the end of each
round.)
1st round (RS) Using B, 1 ch (does NOT count
as a st), 2 dc in first dc, 1 dc in each of next
92 dc, 2 dc in each of next 2 dc, 1 dc in each of
next 92 dc, 2 dc in last dc, change to C and join
with a ss to first ch, turn. *(4 sts increased.)*
2nd round Using C, 1 ch, 2 dc in first dc, 1 dc in
each of next 94 dc, 2 dc in each of next 2 dc,
1 dc in each of next 94 dc, 2 dc in last dc,
change to A and join with a ss to first ch, turn.
(4 sts increased.)

3rd round Using A, 1 ch, 2 dc in first dc, 1 dc in
each of next 96 dc, 2 dc in each of next 2 dc,
1 dc in each of next 96 dc, 2 dc in last dc, join
with a ss to first ch, turn. *(4 sts increased.)*
4th round Using A, 1 ch, 2 dc in first dc, 1 dc in
each of next 98 dc, 2 dc in each of next 2 dc,
1 dc in each of next 98 dc, 2 dc in last dc,
change to B and join with a ss to first ch, turn.
(4 sts increased.)
These 4 rounds form the stripe sequence of
[1 row B, 1 row C, 2 rows A] repeated and set
the positions for the increases.
Cont as now set with stripe sequence and
increases (increasing 4 sts in each round) for
13 rounds more, ending with one round in B.
Fasten off.

TO FINISH
Press lightly on wrong side, following instructions
on yarn label.
Fold scarf in half lengthways with wrong sides
together and sew together around outside edge.
Sew on two poppers where scarf crosses as
shown (see page 93).
Sew button on top of poppers for decoration.

HENRI ELEPHANT

Henri is happiest when he can stand quietly under shady trees with his friend and listen to parrots and monkeys singing. Try making him in different colours – he is very quick and easy to crochet. He prefers to wear his blanket, winter or summer, as he is particularly fond of stars.

BEFORE YOU BEGIN

SIZE
The finished toy elephant measures approximately 20.5cm/8in long by 16.5cm/6½in tall.

YARN
Rowan *Pure Wool DK* (50g/1¾oz balls) as follows:
Green Elephant

A light green (Avocado 019)	2 balls
B light turquoise (Pier 006)	1 ball
C red (Kiss 036)	1 ball
D steel blue (Cypress 007)	1 ball

Blue Elephant

A steel blue (Cypress 007)	2 balls
B light turquoise (Pier 006)	1 ball
C gold (Honey 033)	1 ball
D red (Kiss 036)	1 ball

HOOK
3.50mm (US size E-4) crochet hook

EXTRAS
2 small buttons 11mm/⁷⁄₁₆in in diameter
Toy filling

TENSION
20 sts and 24 rows to 10cm/4in measured over dc using 3.50mm (US size E-4) crochet hook *or size necessary to obtain correct tension.*

ABBREVIATIONS
dc2tog = [insert hook in next st, yrh and draw a loop through] twice, yrh and draw through all 3 loops on hook – *one st decreased.*
See also page 110.

GETTING STARTED

BODY – LEFT SIDE Ⓐ
Each side of the elephant's body is worked from the top of the back to the feet.
Using 3.50mm (US size E-4) hook and A, make 21 ch.
Foundation row (RS) 1 dc in 2nd ch from hook, 1 dc in each of rem ch, turn. *20 dc.*
Row 1 1 ch (does NOT count as a st), 2 dc in each of first 2 dc, 1 dc in each dc to last 2 dc, 2 dc in each of last 2 dc, turn. *24 dc.*
To help keep track of which is RS of piece, after turning work and before beg next row, mark this side of work as RS with a coloured thread.
Row 2 (RS) Rep row 1. *28 dc.*
Row 3 1 ch, 2 dc in first dc, 1 dc in each dc to last 2 dc, 2 dc in each of last 2 dc, turn. *31 dc.*
Row 4 1 ch, 2 dc in first dc, 1 dc in each dc to last dc, 2 dc in last dc, turn. *33 dc.*
Rows 5 and 6 [Rep row 4] twice. *37 dc.*
Row 7 1 ch, 1 dc in each dc to last dc, 2 dc in last dc, turn. *38 dc.*
Row 8 Rep row 4. *40 dc.*
Row 9 1 ch, 1 dc in each dc to end, turn.
Row 10 Rep row 4. *42 dc.*
Row 11 Rep row 9.
Row 12 1 ch, 2 dc in first dc, 1 dc in each dc to end, turn. *43 dc.*
Row 13 Rep row 9.
Row 14 Rep row 12. *44 dc.*
Row 15 Rep row 9.
Row 16 Rep row 12. *45 dc.*
Rows 17–21 [Rep row 9] 5 times.

Trunk
Row 22 (RS) 1 ch, 1 dc in each of first 8 dc, turn. *8 dc.*
Working on these sts only for trunk, cont as follows:
Row 23 1 ch, 1 dc in first dc, work dc2tog over next 2 dc, 1 dc in each dc to end, turn. *7 dc.*
Rows 24–30 [Rep row 9] 7 times.
Fasten off.

Body

With RS facing, cont with body by rejoining A to sts left unworked as follows:

Row 22 (RS) Miss next dc and rejoin A with a ss to next dc, 1 ch, 1 dc in same place as ss, 1 dc in each dc to end, turn. *36 dc.*

Row 23 1 ch, 1 dc in each dc to last 3 dc, work dc2tog over next 2 dc, 1 dc in last dc, turn. *35 dc.*

Rows 24 and 25 [Rep row 9] twice.

Front leg

Row 26 (RS) 1 ch, 1 dc in each of first 12 dc, turn. *12 dc.*

Working on these sts only for front leg, cont as follows:

Row 27 1 ch, 1 dc in first dc, work dc2tog over next 2 dc, 1 dc in each dc to end, turn. *11 dc.*

Row 28 1 ch, 1 dc in each dc to last 3 dc, work dc2tog over next 2 dc, 1 dc in last dc, turn. *10 dc.*

Rows 29–35 [Rep row 9] 7 times. Fasten off.

Back leg

With RS facing, work back leg by rejoining A to sts left unworked as follows:

Row 26 (RS) Miss next 11 dc, rejoin A with a ss to next dc, 1 ch, 1 dc in first same place as ss, 1 dc in each of last 11 dc, turn. *12 dc.*

Row 27 1 ch, 1 dc in each dc to last 3 dc, work dc2tog over next 2 dc, 1 dc in last dc, turn. *11 dc.*

Row 28 1 ch, 1 dc in first dc, work dc2tog over next 2 dc, 1 dc in each dc to end, turn. *10 dc.*

Rows 29–35 [Rep row 9] 7 times. Fasten off.

BODY – RIGHT SIDE Ⓑ

Using 3.50mm (US size E-4) hook and A, make 21 ch.

Foundation row (RS) 1 dc in 2nd ch from hook, 1 dc in each of rem ch, turn. 20 *dc*.

Row 1 1 ch (does NOT count as a st), 2 dc in each of first 2 dc, 1 dc in each dc to last 2 dc, 2 dc in each of last 2 dc, turn. 24 *dc*.

To help keep track of which is RS of piece, after turning work and before beg next row, mark this side of work as RS with a coloured thread.

Row 2 (RS) Rep row 1. 28 *dc*.

Row 3 1 ch, 2 dc in each of first 2 dc, 1 dc in each dc to last dc, 2 dc in last dc, turn. 31 *dc*.

Row 4 1 ch, 2 dc in first dc, 1 dc in each dc to last dc, 2 dc in last dc, turn. 33 *dc*.

Rows 5 and 6 [Rep row 4] twice. 37 *dc*.

Row 7 1 ch, 2 dc in first dc, 1 dc in each dc to end, turn. 38 *dc*.

Row 8 Rep row 4. 40 *dc*.

Row 9 1 ch, 1 dc in each dc to end, turn.

Row 10 Rep row 4. 42 *dc*.

Row 11 Rep row 9.

Row 12 1 ch, 1 dc in each dc to last dc, 2 dc in last dc, turn. 43 *dc*.

Row 13 Rep row 9.

Row 14 Rep row 12. 44 *dc*.

Row 15 Rep row 9.

Row 16 Rep row 12. 45 *dc*.

Rows 17–21 [Rep row 9] 5 times.

Legs

Row 22 (RS) 1 ch, 1 dc in each of first 36 dc, turn. 36 *dc*.

Working on these sts only for legs section, cont as follows:

Row 23 1 ch, 1 dc in first dc, work dc2tog over next 2 dc, 1 dc in each dc to end, turn. 35 *dc*.

Rows 24 and 25 [Rep row 9] twice.

Back leg

Row 26 1 ch, 1 dc in each of first 12 dc, turn. 12 *dc*.

Working on these sts only for back leg, cont as follows:

Row 27 1 ch, 1 dc in first dc, work dc2tog over next 2 dc, 1 dc in each dc to end, turn. 11 *dc*.

Row 28 1 ch, 1 dc in each dc to last 3 dc, work dc2tog over next 2 dc, 1 dc in last dc, turn. 10 *dc*.

Rows 29–35 [Rep row 9] 7 times.
Fasten off.

Front leg

With RS facing, work front leg by rejoining A to sts left unworked as follows:

Row 26 (RS) Miss next 11 dc and rejoin A with a ss to next dc, 1 ch, 1 dc in same place as ss, 1 dc in each of next 11 dc, turn. 12 *dc*.

Working on these sts only for front leg, cont as follows:

Row 27 1 ch, 1 dc in each dc to last 3 dc, work dc2tog over next 2 dc, 1 dc in last dc, turn. 11 *dc*.

Row 28 1 ch, 1 dc in first dc, work dc2tog over next 2 dc, 1 dc in each dc to end, turn. 10 *dc*.

Rows 29–35 [Rep row 9] 7 times.
Fasten off.

Trunk

With RS facing, work trunk by rejoining A to sts left unworked as follows:

Row 22 (RS) Miss next dc and rejoin A with a ss to next dc, 1 ch, 1 dc in same place as ss, 1 dc in each dc to end, turn. 8 *dc*.

Row 23 1 ch, 1 dc in each dc to last 3 dc, work dc2tog over next 2 dc, 1 dc in last dc, turn. 7 *dc*.

Rows 24–30 [Rep row 9] 7 times.
Fasten off.

UNDERBODY C

The underbody forms the belly, the insides of the legs and the underside of the trunk, and it is worked from the back legs to the trunk.

Inside of back legs

Using 3.50mm (US size E-4) hook and A, make 31 ch.

Foundation row (RS) 1 dc in 2nd ch from hook, 1 dc in each of rem ch, turn. 30 *dc*.

Row 1 (patt row) 1 ch (does NOT count as a st), 1 dc in each dc to end, turn.
(Last row forms simple dc patt when repeated.)
Cont in dc throughout, work 8 rows more, ending with a WS row.
Fasten off.

Shape belly

With RS facing, rejoin A and shape belly as follows:

Next row (RS) Miss first 8 dc and rejoin A with a ss to next dc, 1 ch, 1 dc in same place as ss, 1 dc in each of next 13 dc, turn. 14 *dc*.

Next row 1 ch, work dc2tog over first 2 dc, 1 dc in each dc to last 2 dc, work dc2tog over last 2 dc, turn.

Rep last row once more. *10 dc.*

Work straight for 10 rows, ending with a RS row.

Next row (WS) 1 ch, 2 dc in first dc, 1 dc in each dc to last dc, 2 dc in last dc, turn. *12 dc.*

Next row 1 ch, 2 dc in first dc, 1 dc in each dc to last dc, 2 dc in last dc, turn. *14 dc.*

Do not cut off yarn or fasten off, but set aside while you make a length of ch for one leg.

Inside of front legs

Using 3.50mm (US size E-4) hook and a separate length of A, make 8 ch for front leg.

Fasten off.

Return to belly and cont as follows:

Next row (WS) 9 ch, 1 dc in 2nd ch from hook, 1 dc in each of rem 7 ch, 1 dc in each dc to end, then work 1 dc in each of 8 ch just made. *30 dc.*

Work straight for 9 rows, ending with a RS row.

Fasten off.

Shape trunk

With WS facing, rejoin A and work trunk as follows:

Next row (WS) Miss first 13 dc and rejoin A with a ss to next dc, 1 ch, 1 dc in same place as ss, 1 dc in each of next 3 dc, turn. *4 dc.*

Work straight for 4 rows.

Next row 1 ch, [work dc2tog over next 2 dc] twice, turn. *2 dc.*

Work straight for 6 rows.

Fasten off.

OUTER EARS D (make 2)

Using 3.50mm (US size E-4) hook and A, make 13 ch.

Foundation row (RS) 1 dc in 2nd ch from hook, 1 dc in each of rem ch, turn. *12 dc.*

Row 1 (patt row) 1 ch (does NOT count as a st), 1 dc in each dc to end, turn.

Cont in dc throughout, work 2 rows more, ending with a WS row.

Next row (RS) 1 ch, work dc2tog over first 2 dc, 1 dc in each dc to last 2 dc, work dc2tog over last 2 dc, turn. *10 dc.*

Work straight for 2 rows.

Next row (dec row) 1 ch, work dc2tog over first 2 dc, 1 dc in each dc to last 2 dc, work dc2tog over last 2 dc, turn.

Work straight for 1 row.

Rep last 2 rows once more and then dec row again. *4 dc.*

Fasten off.

INNER EARS E (make 2)

Using 3.50mm (US size E-4) hook and B, make 12 ch.

Foundation row (RS) 1 dc in 2nd ch from hook, 1 dc in each of rem ch, turn. *11 dc.*

Row 1 (patt row) 1 ch (does NOT count as a st), 1 dc in each dc to end, turn.

Cont in dc throughout, work 1 row more.

Next row (dec row) 1 ch, work dc2tog over first 2 dc, 1 dc in each dc to last 2 dc, work dc2tog over last 2 dc, turn.

Work straight for 2 rows.

Rep dec row. *7 dc.*

Work straight for 1 row.

Rep dec row. *5 dc.*

Next row 1 ch, work dc2tog over first 2 dc, 1 dc in next dc, work dc2tog over last 2 dc. *3 dc.*

Fasten off.

TAIL F

Using 3.50mm (US size E-4) hook and B, make 13 ch.

Foundation round (RS) 1 dc in 2nd ch from hook, 1 dc in each of rem 11 ch, then working along other side of foundation ch, work 1 dc in each of next 12 ch, do not turn. *24 dc.*

Round 1 (RS) 1 ch, 1 dc in each of first 12 dc, 1 ch, 1 dc in each of last 12 dc, join with a ss to first dc.

Rep last round twice more.

Fasten off.

BLANKET G

Using 3.50mm (US size E-4) hook and D, make 20 ch.

Foundation row (RS) 1 dc in 2nd ch from hook, 1 dc in next ch, *1 ch, miss 1 ch, 1 dc in next ch; rep from * to last ch, 1 dc in last ch, turn. *19 sts.*

Patt row 1 1 ch (does NOT count as a st), 1 dc in first dc, *1 ch, 1 dc in next 1-ch sp; rep from * to last 2 dc, 1 ch, 1 dc in last dc, turn.

Patt row 2 1 ch, 1 dc in first dc, *1 dc in next
1-ch sp, 1 ch; rep from * to last 1-ch sp, 1 dc in
last 1-ch sp, 1 dc in last dc, turn.

(Last 2 rows form patt when repeated.)

Work 43 rows more in patt, ending with a patt
row 1.

Fasten off.

Edging

With RS facing and using 3.50mm (US size E-4)
hook and C, work edging as follows:

Round 1 (RS) Join yarn with a ss to first dc of
previous row, 1 ch, 1 dc in same place as ss, then
work in patt as set across row and cont working
1 ch, 1 dc evenly down side-edge of blanket,
along foundation row of blanket and up other
side-edge, join with a ss to first top of first dc.
Fasten off.

STARS ⊕ (make 2)

Using 3.50mm (US size E-4) hook and C, make
2 ch.

Round 1 (RS) 5 dc in 2nd ch from hook, join with
a ss to first dc.

(Do not turn at end of rounds, but work with RS
always facing.)

Round 2 1 ch, 2 dc same place as ss, 2 dc in each
of rem 4 dc, join with a ss to first dc. *10 dc.*

Round 3 1 ch, 1 dc in same place as ss, 5 ch, 1 ss
in 2nd ch from hook, 1 dc in next ch, 1 htr in next
ch, 1 tr in next ch, 1 tr in same place as first dc,
miss next dc of previous round, *1 dc in next dc,
5 ch, 1 ss in 2nd ch from hook, 1 dc in next ch,
1 htr in next ch, 1 tr in next ch, 1 tr in same place
as first dc of this star point, miss next dc of
previous round; rep from * 3 times more, join
with a ss to first dc. Fasten off.

TASSELS ❶ (make 11)

Using C, wind yarn five times around a piece of
cardboard 5cm/2in wide.

Thread a length of matching yarn onto a blunt-
ended yarn needle and use this length of yarn to
tie together strands of yarn at one end of
cardboard; knot securely, leaving two long tail-
ends of yarn at top of tassel.

Cut through strands at other end of cardboard.

Wrap one tail-end several times around tassel,
1.5cm/½in from top, and secure. (Leave
remaining tail-end at top, for sewing to blanket.)
Trim tassel to 4cm/1½in long.

Make five more tassels using C, and five tassels
using B — for a total of 11 tassels.

TO FINISH

Press pieces lightly on wrong side, following
instructions on yarn label.

Body

With right sides together, join top seam of body
pieces, leaving 7cm/2¾in open along back legs
and 1cm/½in open along front of trunk.

Leaving 7cm/2¾in open along one back leg
seam, sew underbody in place.

Turn right-side out, insert toy filling and sew
openings in seams closed.

Ears

With wrong sides together, sew inner ear pieces
to outer ear pieces.

With inner ears facing forwards, sew one side-
edge of each ear to elephant so that foundation-
chain edge faces outwards.

Eyes

Using a blunt-ended yarn needle and B, work a
large French knot for each eye as shown.

Tail

Fold tail in half lengthways, and sew edges
together. Sew tail to elephant as shown.

Sew one tassel in B to end of tail.

Blanket

Using a blunt-ended yarn needle and C,
embroider four simple cross stitches widthways
across centre of blanket, each worked over two
rows and one stitch apart.

Using B, embroider a large French knot at centre
of each cross stitch.

Sew blanket to elephant, stitching along edges
of blanket and for about 5cm/2in in each
direction from centre back seam.

Sew one star to blanket on each side of
elephant by stitching a button to centre of each
star through both thicknesses.

ZIGZAG THROW

Bold, cheerful, warm and cosy, the Zigzag Throw is perfect for brightening up any winter's day. Easily and quickly made in two pieces, this gorgeous throw needs to be taken out and shown off!

BEFORE YOU BEGIN

SIZE
The finished throw measures approximately 106cm/41¾in wide by 131cm/51½in long, including the edging.

YARN
Rowan *Pure Wool DK* (50g/1¾oz balls) as follows:

A	light turquoise (Pier 006)	11 balls
B	red (Kiss 036)	4 balls
C	mid green (Parsley 020)	3 balls
D	gold (Honey 033)	4 balls
E	orange (Tangerine 040)	2 balls

HOOK
3.50mm (US size E-4) crochet hook

TENSION
Approximately 22 sts and 9 rows to 10cm/4in measured over patt using 3.50mm (US size E-4) crochet hook *or size necessary to obtain correct tension.*

ABBREVIATIONS
tr2tog = [yrh and insert hook in next st, yrh and draw a loop through, yrh and draw a loop through 2 loops on hook] twice, yrh and draw through all 3 loops on hook — *one st decreased.* See also page 110.

GETTING STARTED

FIRST HALF OF THROW
The throw is made in two pieces joined together at the centre.
Using 3.50mm (US size E-4) hook and B, make 225 ch.

Foundation row (RS) 3 tr in 4th ch from hook, *1 tr in each of next 5 ch, [tr2tog over next 2 ch] 3 times, 1 tr in each of next 5 ch, 4 tr in next ch; rep from * to end, turn.
Cut off B.
Change to A.
Row 1 (patt row) 3 ch, miss first 3 tr, 3 tr in next tr, *1 tr in each of next 5 tr, [tr2tog over next 2 tr] 3 times, 1 tr in each of next 5 tr, 4 tr in next tr; rep from *, working last 4 tr in 3rd of 3-ch, turn.
(Last row forms patt when repeated.)
Cont in patt throughout, work 6 rows more A, 1 row C, 1 row D, 1 row E, 1 row D, 1 row C, 7 rows A, 1 row C, 1 row D, 1 row E, 1 row D, 1 row C, 7 rows A, 1 row C, 1 row D, 1 row B, 1 row D, 1 row C, 5 rows A, 1 row B, 1 row A, 1 row B, 1 row A, 1 row B, 1 row E, 1 row D, 1 row C, 1 row A, 1 row B.
Next row (dec row) Using B, 3 ch, miss first 3 tr, 2 tr in next tr, *1 tr in each of next 5 tr, [tr2tog over next 2 tr] 3 times, 1 tr in each of next 5 tr, 2 tr in next tr; rep from *, working last 2 tr in 3rd of 3-ch, turn.
Next row (dec row) Using B, 3 ch, miss first 3 tr, *1 tr in each of next 4 tr, [tr2tog over next 2 tr] 3 times, 1 tr in each of next 5 tr; rep from *, working last tr in 3rd of 3-ch, turn.
Next row Using E, 3 ch, miss first tr, 1 tr in each tr to end, 1 tr in 3rd of 3-ch, turn.
Next row Using D, 3 ch, miss first tr, 1 tr in each tr to end, 1 tr in 3rd of 3-ch, turn.
Next row Using A, 3 ch, miss first tr, 1 tr in each tr to end, 1 tr in 3rd of 3-ch, turn.
Fasten off.

SECOND HALF OF THROW
Work exactly as for first half.

TO FINISH
Sew two pieces together along straight edges of last rows.

Edging
With RS facing and using 3.50mm (US size E-4) hook and B, work edging along one side-edge

of throw as follows:

Row 1 (RS) Join B with a ss to beg of one side-edge, work 3 ch, then work a row of tr evenly along row-ends.

Fasten off.

Using B, work a row of tr in same way along other side-edge of throw but do not fasten off, instead cont around edge of throw and work 1 ss in next st (beg of foundation-chain edge), work 3 ch, then work a round of tr around edge, working decreases and increases to match those in patt along foundation-chain edges and 1 tr in each tr along side-edges, join with a ss to 3rd of 3-ch at beg of round.

Press lightly on wrong side, following instructions on yarn label.

CROCHET HOW-TO TIPS

The projects in this book can be worked with a knowledge of only the most basic crochet stitches. None are too difficult for an average crocheter.

Here are some technical tips for beginners. Intermediate and experienced crocheters will find them useful as well if they haven't picked up their hooks for a while.

CHECKING YOUR CROCHET TENSION

Be sure to check your tension before beginning a project. Make a swatch about 15cm/6in square using the recommended yarn and hook size and working the stitch mentioned in Tension section in the pattern. If your swatch has more stitches and rows to 10cm/4in than specified, try again using a larger hook size. If it has fewer stitches and rows to 10cm/4in, try again using a smaller hook size.

Obtaining the correct tension is especially important when you are making a garment, so try your best to match the specified tension before you start it. Tension on small accessories or on motifs being used to make a large blanket or throw is not that important, so beginners are advised to try one of these as their very first project instead of a garment.

MAINTAINING AN EVEN TENSION

Once you start crocheting your project, you may find that your tension varies. Maintaining an even tension in crochet is not as easy as it is with knitting, especially if the fabric is worked entirely in double crochet or half trebles. Even very experienced crocheters sometimes have trouble keeping their double crochet tension the same throughout an entire garment.

With practice your tension will gradually even out. Try concentrating for a while on how

tightly you are holding and releasing the yarn and on how tight or loose the loops feel on the hook as you make them. After concentrating for a several rows, the tension you have on the yarn and the tightness or looseness of the loops will start to become automatic.

If you leave a project for a few weeks and then go back to it, before working on it again, practice on a scrap swatch for about 20 to 30 minutes to get back into an even rhythm with your stitches.

COUNTING YOUR STITCHES

Crochet patterns give a 'stitch count' at the end of some rows. This tells you how many stitches you should have after working that row. Counting your stitches from time to time is much more important with crochet than with knitting since it is easier to make a mistake in crochet.

Where a stitch count appears at the end of the foundation row or the first row after it, it is essential to count your stitches to make sure you have the right number. For double crochet, the turning chain (the chain stitch at the beginning of the row) is not counted as a stitch — only the actual double crochet stitches are counted. For taller stitches, however, the turning chains are counted as the first stitch of the row. This is usually explained clearly in the pattern.

Stitch counts are often given at the end of a row that has increases or decreases. It is not necessary to count your stitches every time a stitch count appears, but they are there in case you need them. Check at least occasionally when increasing and decreasing to make sure you have the right number of stitches.

Even when you are working your crochet straight for many rows and the number of stitches is not changing, for example on a garment up to the armhole or on a scarf, it is worth counting your stitches occasionally. A lapse of concentration is not unusual and happens to all crocheters (no matter what their skill level), and this loss of concentration may cause you to inadvertently miss a stitch, especially at the edges of the crochet.

MARKING THE 'RIGHT SIDE' OF THE CROCHET

Crochet pattern instructions always tell you which is the right side (abbreviated as 'RS') of the fabric. To a beginner, this may seem unimportant when the crochet fabric itself is reversible, but it is often essential in the construction of the accessory or garment.

A good tip is to mark the right side of your crochet at the beginning when it is first mentioned. To do this, tie a short length of coloured thread to the right side. Later in the pattern when the instructions tell you to hold the crochet with the right side facing you or to work a number of centimetres/inches and end with a wrong-side (WS) row, you will be glad the marker is there!

Don't cut off your 'right-side' markers until the crochet is complete because you may need to refer to it when working an edging with the right or wrong side facing you or when sewing something together with the right or wrong sides facing each other.

WORKING CROCHET STRIPES

When changing to a new colour for stripes, you can change at the beginning of the row that uses the new colour, and this is usually what the instructions indicate.

However, a neater result is achieved if you change to the new colour with the last 'yarn round hook' of the previous row. If you do, the first chain in the new row will already be in the new colour.

BLOCKING AND PRESSING CROCHET

Before you stitch together your crochet pieces, you should press them lightly if instructed to do so in the pattern instructions. This is your chance to smooth out handcrafted stitches and gently nudge your garment pieces into a more even shape.

Begin by pinning out each piece wrong-side up to the recommended measurements — this is called blocking. Check the pressing instructions on your yarn label to see if it is possible to press the yarn with a warm iron. If pressing is not recommended, then lay a clean damp cloth over the crochet and leave the cloth and crochet until both are completely dry.

If you can use a warm iron on your yarn, then lay a clean damp cloth over it and gently press the crochet over the damp cloth to create steam. Do not drag or slide the iron over the cloth, but lift it up to move it. Do not press down on the iron when it is in place or leave it too long in one place or you will squash the natural texture of the crochet.

Remove the cloth and leave the crochet until it is completely dry.

SEAMS ON CROCHET

Take your time when finishing your crochet. Don't rush — and don't hesitate to undo seams (or edgings) and start again if they don't look right the first time. It may feel frustrating at the time, but it is worth the extra effort and patience.

Both oversewing stitches and backstitch are good for sewing seams on crochet pieces. Using a blunt-ended yarn needle, test which seam you like best for your accessory or garment by trying it out on two small swatches.

Some crocheters like to work seams with crochet stitches. To do this, hold the pieces with the right sides together and work a line of chain stitches through both layers very close to the edge. Although this is a quick way to join pieces together, it may create a bulkier seam than you want for a child's garment, so be sure to test it before trying it on the garment pieces.

For seams on toys, I find that the best seam to use, where possible, is backstitch — for example, when stitching together the toy's main body pieces. Simply place the right sides together, sew the seam close to the edge with small, even backstitches, then turn right side out.

Perservere and you will find the type of seam that works best for you.

CROCHET ABBREVIATIONS

The following are the abbreviations used in the patterns in this book. Special abbreviations are given with individual patterns.

alt	alternate
beg	begin (ning)
ch	chain
ch sp	chain space
cm	centimetre (s)
cont	continu (e) (ing)
dc	double crochet
dec	decreas (e) (ing)
DK	double knitting (a medium-weight yarn)
foll	follow (s) (ing)
g	gramme (s)
htr	half treble
in	inch (es)
inc	increas (e) (ing)
m	metre (s)
mm	millimetre (s)
oz	ounce (s)
patt	pattern
rem	remain (s) (ing)
rep	repeat (s) (ing)
RS	right side
sp	space
ss	slip stitch
st(s)	stitch (es)
tog	together
tr	treble
WS	wrong side
yd	yard (s)
yrh	yarn round hook

* = Repeat instructions after asterisk or between asterisks as many times as instructed.

[ ] = Repeat instructions inside square brackets as many times as instructed; or work all instructions inside square brackets into same place.

CROCHET TERMINOLOGY

English language crochet terminology is not the same in all countries. This book was written with the crochet terminology used in the United Kingdom. If you have learned crochet using the US terminology, use this list to find the meaning of the UK terms and their abbreviations:

UK	US
slip stitch (ss)	slip stitch (sl st)
double crochet (dc)	single crochet (sc)
half treble crochet (htr)	half double crochet (hdc)
treble crochet (tr)	double crochet (tr)
double treble (dtr)	treble crochet (tr)
triple treble (trtr)	double treble (dtr)
quadruple treble (qtr)	triple treble (trtr)
miss	skip
yarn round hook (yrh)	yarn over hook (yo)

YARN INFORMATION

For the best results, use the yarns recommended in the patterns. The yarns used in this book are Rowan yarns. If, however, you are attempting to use a substitute yarn, be sure to use a yarn that matches the original in type, and buy according to length of yarn per ball, rather than by the weight of the ball.

The specifications of the yarns used in this book are given below. The recommended tension for stocking stitch is given for each yarn because this gives an accurate guide to the thickness of the yarn.

Shade numbers are provided with each crochet pattern, but these are only suggestions. There can be no guarantee that every colour will still be available by the time you use this book, as shades change frequently with fashion trends.

ROWAN COTTON GLACE

A lightweight cotton yarn; 100 per cent cotton; approximately 115m/126yd per 50g/1¾oz ball; recommended tension — 23 sts and 32 rows to 10cm/4in measured over stocking stitch using 3.25—3.75mm (US size 3—5) knitting needles.

ROWAN 4-PLY COTTON

A lightweight cotton yarn; 100 per cent cotton; approximately 170m/186yd per 50g/1¾oz ball; recommended tension — 27—29 sts and 37—39 rows to 10cm/4in measured over stocking stitch using 3—3.25mm (US size 2—3) knitting needles.

ROWAN 4-PLY SOFT

A lightweight wool yarn; 100 per cent merino wool; approximately 175m/191yd per 50g/1¾oz ball; recommended tension — 28 sts and 36 rows to 10cm/4in measured over stocking stitch using 3.25mm (US size 3) knitting needles.

ROWAN PURE WOOL DK

A double-knitting-weight yarn; 100 per cent super-wash wool yarn; approximately 125m/137yd per 50g/1¾oz ball; recommended tension — 22 sts and 30 rows to 10cm/4in measured over stocking stitch using 4mm (US size 6) knitting needles.

YARN ADDRESSES

Contact the distributors listed here to find a supplier of Rowan handknitting yarns near you. For countries not listed, contact the main office in the UK or the Rowan website: **www.knitrowan.com**

UK: Rowan,
Green Lane Mill,
Holmfirth, West Yorkshire HD9 2DX,
England.
Tel: +44 (0) 1484 681881.
Fax: +44 (0) 1484 687920.
E-mail: mail@knitrowan.com

AUSTRALIA: Australian Country Spinners,
314 Albert Street, Brunswick, Victoria 3056.
Tel: (03) 9380 3888.

AUSTRIA: Coats Harlander GmbH,
Autokaderstrasse 31, A-1230 Wien.

Tel: (01) 27716-0.
Fax: (01) 27716-228.

BELGIUM: Coats Benelux,
Ring Oost 14A, Ninove, 9400.
Tel: 054 318989.
E-mail: sales.coatsninove@coats.com

CANADA: Same as USA.

CHINA: Coats Shanghai Ltd.,
No. 9 Building, Doasheng Road,
Songjiang Industrial Zone,
Shanghai.
Tel: 86 21 5774 3733 Ext 329.
Fax: 86 21 5774 3768.
E-mail: victor.li@coats.com

DENMARK: Coats HP A/S,
Nannagade 28, 2200 Copenhagen.

Tel: 35 86 90 50.
Fax: 35 82 15 10.

FINLAND: Coats Opti Oy,
Ketjutie 3, 04220 Kerava.
Tel: (358) 9 274871.
Fax: (358) 9 2748 7330.
E-mail: coatsopti.sales@coats.com
www.coatscrafts.com

FRANCE: Coats Steine,
100 avenue du Général de Gaulle,
18 500 Mehun-Sur-Yèvre.
Tel: 02 48 23 12 30. Fax: 02 48 23 12 40.
www.coatscrafts.fr

GERMANY: Coats GMBH,
Kaiserstrasse 1, D-79341 Kenzingen.
Tel: 07162-14346.
www.coatsgmbh.de

HOLLAND: Coats Benelux,
Ring Oost 14A, Ninove, 9400.
Tel: 0346 35 37 00.
E-mail: sales.coatsninove@coats.com

HONG KONG: Coats China Holding Ltd.,
19/F., Millenium City 2, 378 Kwun Tong Road,
Kwun Tong, Kowloon.
Tel: (852) 2798 6886.
Fax: (852) 2305 0311.
Email: jackie.li@coats.com

ICELAND: Rowan at Storkurinn,
Laugavegi 59, ICE-101.
Tel: 551 8258.

ITALY: dl srl, Via Piave, 24-26,
20016 Pero, Milan.
Tel: 02 339 101 80.

JAPAN: Puppy-Jardin Co. Ltd.,
3-8 11 Kudanminami, Chiyodaku,
Hiei Kudan Bldg. 5F, Tokyo.
Tel: 3222-7076.
Fax: 3222-7066.
E-mail: info@rowan-jaeger.com

KOREA: Coats Korea Co. Ltd.,
5F Kuckdong B/D, 935-40 Bangbae-Dong,
Seocho-Gu, Seoul.
Tel: 82-2-521-6262.
Fax: 82-2-521-5181.

MEXICO: Estambres Crochet SA de CV,
Aaron Saenz 1891-7,
Monterrey, NL 64650.
Tel: +52 (81) 8335-3870.

NEW ZEALAND: ACS New Zealand,
1 March Place, Belfast, Christchurch.
Tel: 64-3-323-6665.
Fax: 64-3-323-6660.

NORWAY: Coats Knappehuset AS,
Pb 100 Ulset, 5873 Bergen.
Tel: (47) 55 53 93 00.
Fax: (47) 55 53 93 93.

SINGAPORE: Golden Dragon Store,
101 Upper Cross Street #02-51,
People's Park Centre,
Singapore 058357.
Tel: (65) 65358454.
E-mail: gdscraft@hotmail.com

SOUTH AFRICA: Arthur Bales Ltd.,
62 4th Avenue, Linden,
Johannesburg 2195.
Tel: (27) 118 882 401.
Fax: (27) 117 826 137.
E-mail: arthurb@new.co. za

SPAIN: Oyambre, Pau Claris 145,
80009 Barcelona.
Tel/Fax: (34) 93 4872672.

SWEDEN: Coats Expotex AB,
Division Craft, Box 297,
401 24 Göteborg.
Tel: (46) 33 720 79 00.
Fax: (46) 31 47 16 50.

SWITZERLAND: Coats Stoppel AG,
CH-5300 Tungi (AG).
Tel: 056 298 12 20.
Fax: 056 298 12 50.

TAIWAN: Laiter Wool Knitting Co. Ltd.,
10-1 313 Lane, Sec 3,
Chung Ching North Road, Taipei.
Tel: (886) 2 2596 0269.
Fax: (886) 2 2598 0619.

THAILAND: Global Wide Trading,
10 Lad Prao Soi 88, Bangkok 10310.
Tel: 00 662 933 9019.
Fax: 00 662 933 9110.

USA: Westminster Fibers Inc.,
165 Ledge Street, Nashua, NH 03060.
Tel: 1-800-445-9276.
E-mail: rowan@westminsterfibers.com
www.westminsterfibers.com

ACKNOWLEDGEMENTS

Many thanks to all who were involved with this book and for all your hard work!
Especially Susan for wise words, wisdom and guidance, Sally and Penny for expertise and patience, and François
for his abounding talent and for making everything look lovely!